PRACTICAL

FOUNDATIONS FOR THE
EARLY YEARS

TEACHING WITHIN THE
NATIONAL CURRICULUM

CAROLINE MATUSIAK

Published by Scholastic Publications Ltd,
Villiers House, Clarendon Avenue,
Leamington Spa, Warwickshire CV32 5PR

© 1992 Scholastic Publications Ltd.
Reprinted 1993

Written by Caroline Matusiak
Edited by Janet Fisher
Sub-edited by Catherine Baker
Designed by Lynne Joesbury
Illustrated by Karen Heywood
Photographs by Peter Corbett

Printed by Ebenezer Baylis, Worcester

Front cover designed by Joy White and Sue Limb
Front cover illustrated by Lynda Taylor

British Library Cataloguing in Publication Data

A catalogue record for this book is available from
the British Library.

ISBN 0-590-53013-5

For Tony

Contents

Chapter 6
Foundation subjects   151

Introduction

The importance of education for under-fives has been recognised for many years, as has the value of building on early skills in the first years of primary education.

'To establish artificial boundaries between the education of children under five and that received by five year olds would be both counter-productive and an opportunity lost. Many of the activities frequently and properly undertaken by children under five will correspond to statements of attainment within the National Curriculum.'
(*Curriculum Guidance 1: A Framework for the Primary Curriculum*, National Curriculum Council 1989.)

A stimulating, well-planned environment such as that found in many nurseries and playgroups provides the range of experiences and activities necessary for children to acquire the attitudes, skills and concepts outlined in the National Curriculum. You need to appraise your work with the children carefully to ensure progression and continuity with later stages of schooling. This also enables you to explain to parents, governors, headteachers and others how current early years practice provides the foundation for the National Curriculum.

This book is intended as a guide to help you to identify subject areas. You may find it also suggests some additional activities which may extend or complement the work you are already doing. The activities are intended as ideas for you to adapt according to the needs and interests of your children. Early years teaching still depends on your resourcefulness and initiative for its effectiveness.

Responsive teaching

'For young children it is usually inappropriate to view the curriculum – from the point of view of the learner – as separate subjects. Young children often learn through collaborative, exploratory, manipulative and imaginative play, but teachers should be aware of what underlies the various activities in which children are engaged.' (*Curriculum Guidance 1*, National Curriculum Council 1989.)

Early years teaching has its own challenges and potential. It is full of promise, enthusiasm and fun. The way you teach is as important as what you teach. Knowing a subject's potential helps you to plan a broad, balanced and integrated curriculum that takes into account children's physical, social, emotional and intellectual development. It gives you confidence to respond to the children's interests and to share your own interests with them. A topic on water, or a child's interest in water, can give rise to science (investigating the properties of water); maths (comparing volume and capacity); and English (introducing the appropriate language and making available the relevant literature, both fact and fiction).

When you become aware of the potential of a subject, you will find ways of extending a topic and introducing more activities to give children the necessary experience. You will be able to intervene in children's play with suitable suggestions or questions. Familiarity with the programmes of study will show you how young children's own interests relate to them. This will give you the confidence to respond to child-initiated learning. Equally, you can continue to bring your own interests into the classroom, aware of how they map on to the National Curriculum. The unexpected event that so often holds children's attention, for example, a sudden storm or a leak in the water tray, can continue to be a vehicle for learning; you will continue to respond to the child and the situation, whether foreseen or unforeseen. Consequently, early years teaching retains its immediacy and its dynamism, which lie in the here and now.

Young children learn through play, by exploring, manipulating, collaborating and imagining. Play is the motivation for both physical and mental activity. It has its own goals, and you need to recognise the implications of this in planning and in responding to children's play. While you may be aware of subject areas, children only want to discover what materials feel like, what they can do and what they are called. Children actively seek a meaning from a situation which demands their whole attention and which has the potential to develop physical, social, intellectual and emotional skills simultaneously. You can intervene to support and extend children's play. In this way, early years education will preserve its essential nature which is rooted in its response to the child as an individual, and is characterised by its freshness and spontaneity.

Links with home

Two very influential worlds for the child are home and school or nursery. The latter does not, indeed cannot, substitute for the former, but it can offer activities that enrich the child's experience and help to develop her potential. There needs to be a dialogue between home and school so that parents can continue in their role as educators. Parents usually welcome information and opportunities to be actively involved, while schools welcome the support that they can bring. Children benefit the most, however, from a mutual understanding between parents and teachers. Parents who are informed about current practice become an asset to their child and to the school. Moreover, they understand that activities and experiences are the key to young children's learning, and appreciate that these lay the foundation for the National Curriculum.

Chapter 1
Planning for play

'For young children, purposeful play is an essential and rich part of the learning process. Play is a powerful motivator, encouraging children to be creative and to develop their ideas, understanding and language.' (DES, *Starting with Quality* [The Rumbold Report], HMSO 1990.)

Children learn a great deal as they play. Watching them play is a fascinating exercise. Attitudes, skills and knowledge are acquired as the child strives to understand the world around him by handling and thinking about it.

Play is both a mental and a physical activity. During play we accumulate knowledge of the world through our five senses and try to make sense of it by thinking about it. For example, we compare and contrast experiences to form a concept or general idea such as 'blue' or 'not blue'. The greater the variety of first-hand material, activities and experiences, the greater the potential for learning.

Play

Play absorbs the whole child. Observe the concentration, involvement and intensity when a child plays. Playing makes physical, social, emotional and intellectual demands on a child. Sometimes all these demands are concurrent, but at other times one area becomes more apparent. Some equipment is designed to develop one aspect; for example, a climbing frame helps to improve physical skills. However, children interpret equipment according to their needs and a climbing frame may also be the source of social, emotional and intellectual development. For this reason, it is important to present children with equipment that is open to interpretation rather than narrowly defined. A climbing frame that can be shared with others and used for imaginative play, offers shapes and spaces to be explored as well as inviting the children to develop a variety of physical skills. It has more to offer young children, who develop skills more easily in context than in isolation.

Play as a vehicle for knowledge

Play is personal to the child. The need for security, friends, physical activity and knowledge accumulates and requires immediate satisfaction, regardless of the circumstances. The younger the child, the more obvious this is. It is often termed egocentricity. As a child matures, he starts to control his emotions and begins to recognise the needs of others. Play is the vehicle for the child's quest for knowledge about himself, others and the world.

Learning to play

Children's ability to play cannot be taken for granted. In order to play the child must have the materials, the curiosity and the confidence to explore. Some children have limited access to materials, some may be discouraged from 'making a mess', while others may feel too overwhelmed by family tensions to be able to express an interest in the world around them. Such children may not be familiar with handling toys and may not know what to do with them. Some children are unwilling to handle clay, paint or paste, while others are so withdrawn that building a sense of security is their prerequisite for play.

One of the most valuable roles you can offer is as a playmate for the children. By playing alongside and with them, you can demonstrate how equipment is used and encourage them to explore. Sharing children's play involves discussing and negotiating a common goal which you can enable children to achieve by helping them to use the equipment.

When confronted with a new object, we all investigate its potential or, rather, 'play' with it. The first time I was confronted with a word processor, I pressed keys, watching the letters appear and disappear. Typing words was secondary to finding out about the potential of the machine and how it worked. It was exploration for its own sake. Later, this became more systematic as I sought to use the machine for a purpose. Exploration provides us with knowledge to use at a later stage. The same processes of exploration are evident in children's play. Children play in different ways with different equipment according to how familiar they are with it.

Characteristics of play

Random exploration

When children are new to nursery or playgroup, they will often pick up objects at random, drop them and move on to something else. Support children by playing alongside them, helping them to realise the potential of equipment and prolonging their concentration.

Practice play

Children will often repeat activities, sometimes over several days, as they consolidate skills and knowledge. This gives them a sense of achievement and the confidence to explore further. Ensure that equipment is available for children to repeat models and activities, according to their need.

Purposeful exploration

As children become familiar with equipment, they approach it with specific ideas of what they intend to do. They will search for particular objects rather than play with whatever is 'on top' or is being used by others. A child may investigate a concept, for example, the idea of enclosure or 'inside' by hiding herself or an object in different areas of the nursery. She may do this by making dens, wrapping packages, making models with figures inside or making pies. Encourage children to discuss their intentions and how they aim to achieve them, and give them new possibilities to try.

Playing to learn

Playing is doing, talking and thinking. The atmosphere and ethos of the nursery help to build the emotional security that children need to explore. Some materials encourage children to express their feelings, for example, clay and sand. By using such equipment children develop a broad range of skills and a love of learning which lays the foundation for future education.

Physical play

• As children move and explore large spaces they develop <u>gross motor skills</u> such as running, hopping and climbing.

Vigorous physical play is essential to healthy growth and active minds.
• Fine motor skills develop as children manipulate equipment, for example, LEGO, jigsaws and jugs, and use tools, for example, in sewing, threading and painting. Many of these activities also develop the hand-eye co-ordination that is essential for writing and reading.

Social play

Playing alongside others provides a marvellous opportunity for children to develop their social skills. Playing with others is a landmark in a child's development, but all children need the opportunity to play alone at times. Children's responses to others in the context of play vary widely.
• Solitary play. On entry to nursery or school, young children often play alone, oblivious of others as they explore equipment.

• Parallel play. Many are happy to play alongside other children, each intent on their own purpose but aware of the other children around them.
• Spectator play. Children watch other children play. This provides a transition between playing on their own and with others. When a child observes others to get to know them and the games they play, he is preparing to join in with their play in the near future. Spectator play usually takes place at a safe distance from others, for example, as the child peers over the top of a book or from behind a corner of the sand-pit.
• Simple co-operative play. Children play alongside each other, talking and exchanging equipment. They are starting to share some games together.
• Complex co-operative play. Children discuss and plan how they will play together. This will involve two or more individuals. The home corner, large construction toys and outdoor facilities encourage children to develop such play, by making demands on their social and communicative skills.

Intellectual play

As children play with others and use equipment they develop cognitive skills. The interest and motivation that accompanies self-directed play encourages a child to concentrate and persevere.

Talking is a bridge between doing and thinking. It puts experiences and activities into words that can be recalled to compare and contrast what children have been doing, laying the foundation for concept development. Being able to talk about objects and experiences takes a child out of the here and now and enables him to manipulate thoughts and ideas creatively.

As children develop, they learn to deal with abstract concepts and ideas out of context. Play offers experiences that help them move from concrete to abstract thinking. During the early years, children learn symbolic systems such as talking, mark-making and modelling. These lay the

foundations for future work in English, maths, science and technology.

Communicating

Communication is the key to playing with others. Discussing and planning together gives children the opportunity to become aware of the ideas of others. This encourages children to express and refine their own ideas. Talking, role-playing, reading stories, mark-making, movement, dance, painting, music and modelling all offer ways of communicating for children to explore.

Imagining

Children's explorations become the foundation for imagining all sorts of situations. Stories introduce the world of the imagination where all things are possible. At first, children enjoy stories that relate to their everyday life. Later, they develop a thirst for fantasy, and make-believe creatures such as those in *Where the Wild Things Are* by Maurice Sendak (Bodley Head/Puffin) become part of their imaginative play. Supplying undefined play equipment, for example, a building shell rather than a fully-equipped garage, encourages children to use their own imagination.

Representing

Initially, children explore paint and other materials in terms of their texture, colour and appearance. Later, they use them to represent other things, for example, they may paint a man or make a boat. Do not expect all children to be able to represent something else. As we pretended to be rabbits during a movement session, one child called out, 'I'm not a rabbit. I'm a boy'. Most children have no problems with this, but we should give all children the opportunity to represent objects and experiences. Templates and teacher-

directed modelling are not the answer. Indeed, they may give children the idea that only adult representation is valid. Only by observing how the child uses materials, and listening to what he says, can we know whether or not he can represent. First 'drawings' are personal and their subject is often indistinguishable to an adult eye, but we must always praise children's work and encourage them.

Problem-solving

The ability to solve problems depends on being able to devise alternative solutions. It also demands perseverance and a willingness to investigate new methods.

Reasoning

A stimulating environment encourages children to be curious, as they investigate why things happen. This motivates them to repeat and test an activity. In fact, they are seeking causal links, looking for order and pattern in events. As they reason, children draw on their experience. For example, the snail stays on the side of the tank, 'because of its sticky-tape tummy'. The use of the word 'because' shows the child is starting to reason.

How children learn

Young children learn by interacting with their environment, with their peers and with adults. Learning is a creative process in which children actively make sense of the world around them. As they learn, they use all five senses and their imagination. Experiences and activities provide children with the opportunity to develop their knowledge, skills and attitudes in a meaningful way.

Young children look for causal links in their experience. However, their conclusions may differ from an adult's as they are based on limited experience. Young children do not merely imitate but reinvent systems, for example, writing. Children search for reasons and their own mark-making reflects their level of understanding of writing. At first, it may simply be a zigzag line or a row of circles, which indicates that they are aware of the difference between drawing and writing. Later they produce recognisable letter shapes, demonstrating their understanding that letters have a specific shape.

Young children's learning can be defined in many ways.

- It is active. They discover by actively exploring their environment and testing ideas.
- It is sensory. Information is channelled through the five senses and children need a wide range of experiences to form and refine their concepts or ideas about the world.
- It is concerned with making sense of the world. Children look for patterns and reasons in order to understand a situation. Activities need to be meaningful and set in context.
- It is imitative. Young children follow the role models offered by adults. They are influenced by the 'hidden curriculum', that is, what people *actually* do, as well as by what they say they do. One example is reading, where an adult's enjoyment of books is reflected in the child's interest in books, as well as in her reading behaviour.
- It is creative. Children not only imitate but re-create their understanding in a meaningful context, for example, by making marks on paper as a 'letter for mummy'.
- It is individual. Each child makes his own sense of the experiences, activities and attitudes he encounters. Just as young children's early representation is personal, so is their understanding of the world. For this reason, you need to work with each child individually to support self-directed learning.
- It is social. Young children learn by negotiating or discussing ideas with others as they play. This helps them to define, express and refine their own concepts.
- It is a process of apprenticeship. Young children learn through the attention, support and challenge of an adult sharing their play.

The teacher's role

The teacher is a facilitator of learning. An early years teacher has to be receptive to young children's needs and respond accordingly. Her role includes managing the learning environment and co-ordinating the team of people working with the children. It involves providing materials and enabling children to achieve their potential. She must think about the teaching in terms of the content, or *what* is taught, and the teaching approach, or *how* this is achieved; both are equally important in the early years. Essentially, the teacher's role involves planning, observing, evaluating, interacting and record-keeping.

Planning

Planning for learning through play

Children need the opportunity to explore materials, create their own artefacts and practise skills. As the nursery environment is the vehicle for learning, you must plan equipment, space and time carefully. Before you do this, get down to child height and look around. Is anything out of vision or reach? Planning for learning should be continually evaluated to match the needs of the current children.

The role of play in learning

Equipment

When considering equipment, it may be useful to ask yourself the following questions.

• Is the equipment capable of being used in an open-ended way so that children develop imagination as well as physical skills? Open-ended use of equipment encourages planning and problem-solving as children determine the course or the outcome of play.

• Does it offer a variety of activities that involve the whole child and cater for his social, emotional, physical and intellectual development?

• Does it support a broad and balanced curriculum including all areas of learning?

• Does your equipment offer a variety of sensory experience, for example, different textures, temperatures, tastes, sounds, smells and sights? Include all five senses and draw children's attention to the different sense experiences that objects bring, for example, the taste, smell, texture and colour of a lemon.

• Does your equipment offer different sizes and shapes to develop fine and gross motor skills? Equipment of different shapes and sizes will also develop understanding of space and shape.

• Does it encourage children to plan and play together? For example, a large selection of construction materials allows several children to work together or alongside each other.

• Does the equipment encourage independence? Children need to be able to select and choose equipment without your help. Toilets and sinks, for example, need to be at child height.

Space

When assessing the use of space in your nursery or school, consider the following points.

• Does it encourage independence, giving easy access to all facilities?

• Is the use of space constant, so that children become familiar with the layout and arrangement of materials? This enables them to return to objects they have used and plan their next activity. When furniture is frequently moved around, children are unable to remember where things are and a large amount of time may be spent searching rather than doing.

• Is the equipment arranged in meaningful units, for example, mark-making materials in the 'office'?

• Is there easy access to a low sink so that children can help with setting out and tidying away paint and scrap materials?

• Is there somewhere for children to run and jump?

• Is there somewhere for children to be quiet?

• Does the layout of rooms focus children's attention on the activities or are they continually distracted by other children?

• Does the arrangement encourage children to play with each other and share equipment?

• Is there a heavy duty non-slip floor covering so that sand, water, clay and paint activities can be carried out safely?

• Is there space to save models that children have been working on and wish to complete at a later date?

Areas of activity

Arranging the space into distinct areas provides children with a familiar layout, so that they know where to locate and replace materials. The number of areas will depend on the size of the nursery or classroom, but the list below features the basic areas.

• Paint. Include ready-mixed and powder paint. Leave it near to the scrap materials to encourage children to paint models.

• A water tray and equipment.

• A sand tray and equipment.

• A food area.

• A writing or office area, with access to a word processor if possible.

• Construction. Include large blocks, crates and planks; small equipment with a variety of fastenings, such as LEGO, Mobilo, bricks and Brio Mec; scrap materials and ways of fixing them together, for example, paste, wool and tape; jigsaws, mosaics and other activities that encourage exploration of space, shape and pattern.

• A role-play area with furniture, clothes and equipment for a variety of settings.

• Dough and clay.

• A music area with instruments and song-books.

• A book corner with stories, non-fiction, poetry and rhymes.

• An outdoor area with space and equipment for developing gross motor skills.

• An investigation table where children can closely observe different objects.

Time

• Is there a member of staff free at the beginning of the session to welcome each child?

• Is most of the time devoted to self-directed activities, with children planning, carrying out and completing activities for themselves?

• Is there time for sharing activities as a group, for example, stories, songs, rhymes, music and games?

• Are transitions between activities kept to a minimum, for example, changes from self-directed to group activity? Are children and staff able to make the transitions as smooth as possible?

• Is the routine familiar to children so that they have an awareness of time passing, which gives them a sense of security? The routine does not have to be inflexible, however. Be ready on the spur of the moment to incorporate an activity that captures children's interest.

• Do you give children time to think and reflect or are they continually rushed from one activity to another?

• Is the team familiar with rotas so that everyone can carry out his or her duties efficiently?

Planning for topics

Many early years teachers find topics a useful way of introducing new activities and ideas. Topics are designed to extend children's horizons. They are a vehicle for integrated learning, providing stimulating activities that encourage language, maths, science and technology – often simultaneously. Topics can arise through your initiative, or from children's interests, for example, finding minibeasts and wanting to know more about them. The duration of topic work depends on children's interest and on your ability to extend it in a meaningful way.

You should always consider a topic as a means of awakening children's own interests. These interests often bring a new slant to the familiar, and determine the course of topics. Plan activities for each area of the classroom, including a discovery centre, and include visits and visitors. Subject areas for each activity can be identified according to National Curriculum guidelines when you are planning, perhaps using the abbreviations En for English, Ma for maths and Sc for science. However, the way you identify subject areas in a topic will be based on how you intend to approach each activity. A child may respond to the activities you provide in an unexpected yet equally valid way.

Planning for individuals

You have to be aware of the needs of individual children in order to plan an appropriate curriculum. Children with special needs often receive attention simultaneously from several sources, for example, a physiotherapist, an occupational therapist, a speech therapist and an educational psychologist. You may need to consult with the relevant agencies to co-ordinate an effective programme for the children. Ensure that non-teaching assistants working with the children are kept up-to-date with recent developments and have the opportunity to contribute to records.

Planning as a team

It is important to plan the teaching as a team. This ensures that as many ideas as possible are considered and that all staff understand the aims and objectives of the curriculum. Discuss teaching approaches and child management issues so that staff act consistently. These issues determine the ethos and atmosphere of the classroom.

Planning for parents

Many conversations with parents are informal, but you need to ensure that there are opportunities for parents to speak to you. Parents and other helpers also need to know what their role is and where to seek help, should they need it. Keeping parents informed about classroom topics and events offers them a chance to participate.

Observing

Observation tells you a great deal about young children's needs and their responses to classroom activities. It is the root of planning, interacting, evaluation and record-keeping. To teach effectively, you need to watch and listen closely as the children play.

A focus for observation

It is important to have a focus for observation. This may be:
• an individual child, to observe either general development or an area of concern;
• a group of children, to observe their interaction, a selection of their activities and their social relationships;
• an activity, to observe how children respond to it;
• an area of the classroom, for example, the construction toys. Which children visit it? Which equipment is used? How? Are there implications for future resourcing or resiting of equipment? Is the area dominated by one group or one sex? If so, how can this be overcome?

What to look and listen for

Looking

Look closely at the way the child does an activity to assess her physical skills and the nature of her play.

• What is she doing?
• What equipment is she using and how?
• Is there a sequence of activities, for example, filling a jug and pouring?
• Is this repeated with different equipment, for example, a pan, a spoon or a jug?
• Is this repeated with similar equipment, for example, a pan, a jug and a lipped container?
• How long does the child spend in this area?
• Does she move off to another activity with a sense of purpose?

Listening

Listen to the child to gain an idea about his social relationships and language development.
• Who else is in the area? Are they playing together or independently?

• Is the child talking with another person? If so, is it an adult or a child?

• Are both contributing to the conversation?

• Are children planning the activity together?

• Are they co-operating? Are they playing alongside each other with or without talking?

• Listen as the child talks. Does he use one- or two-word phrases, simple or complex statements? That is, does he express a single idea or several? Write down an extract of the conversation.

Developing a system

You will need to find a way of observing that is appropriate and effective in your classroom. There are two essential points. Firstly, involve all staff, as they will bring an invaluable variety of perspectives on a child or activity. Secondly, have a notepad and pencil nearby as significant events and words are easily forgotten.

To be effective and ongoing, observation needs to become part of the routine. This could be done in either of two ways.

• Ask all the staff to observe a child as she plays. At the end of the session, compare notes and piece together the whole picture.

• Ask the staff to observe an area in turn. This could coincide with their duty in that area. At the end of the rota, compare notes and evaluate how the area is used.

Interacting

How you intervene in children's play depends on the areas of need you have identified during observation. These needs may be general, for example, a child may lack confidence, or they may be specific to the present activity, for example, children

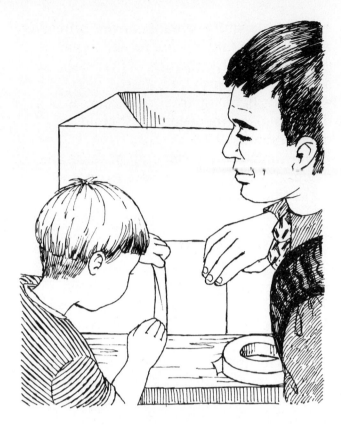

may need help with fastening materials together. You should know your children and interact according to their needs.

Some reasons for intervention

• It can support the child's self-directed activity. Intervention in this case implies showing an interest in what the child is trying to do. Your presence may be sufficient to show that the activity is valued. Talk about what the child is doing.
• Intervention can be used to sustain the child's interest in an activity. You may have to offer help to overcome physical limitations or suggest alternatives when something has not worked: 'Let's think what else we can do...'.
• By intervening you can extend the activity. This may involve offering challenges, for example, 'Can you make your car move?', or, 'What else can we use for making a car?'
• You can intervene to help in language development. Children often need to express in words what they are doing. They require conversation partners who will listen to them and introduce the relevant language.

However, it is important to remember that there are times when you should make a deliberate decision not to intervene and to remain silent. There are also times when children need to be left to concentrate and work independently.

Evaluating

Evaluation needs to be systematic and continuous. All areas of nursery experience require evaluation to ensure that they match the changing needs of the children. Observation and interaction provide information about children and their responses to activities, and this will help you determine whether or not the children's needs are being met. Evaluation is the key to effective planning.

Areas to evaluate

The whole learning environment

This includes the use of materials, space and time, as well as the following important factors.
• Are children interested?
• Are they concentrating?
• Are they playing together?
• Are all areas of learning provided for?
• Are materials well maintained?
• Are children encouraged to work independently?

Staff interaction

• Are you helping children to realise their potential?
• Are you listening to children?
• How can you help individuals?
• Are your efforts effective?
• Does your presence sustain an activity or distract the child?
• What else can you try?

Record-keeping

Staff observation and interaction provide the basis for record-keeping. Records need to be manageable for those who keep them and comprehensible to those who use them. They need to be useful, simple and appropriate.

Reasons for record-keeping

The following list details some of the advantages of keeping records.

• They help you to monitor a child's progress, describing her social, emotional, physical and intellectual development. This helps you to diagnose any specific problems and enables you to plan for individual needs.

• They will provide information for the relevant authorities that will help them to understand the child better.

• Records facilitate continuity and progression in the next stage of education.

• They help staff evaluate current provision and practice. In this way, records assist the planning and organisation of materials and areas of learning.

• Records help you involve parents in observing and recording their child's development.

• They help ensure that staff observe and discuss each child. The discussion is as important as the recording.

Types of record

There are two main types of record. One charts developmental features of early learning while the other, the profile, describes the individual characteristics. Some classrooms use one or the other method exclusively. However, these two forms of record-keeping complement each other and it is worthwhile to include both types. Examples of recording charts are included on pages 50, 89, 150 and 176.

The chart

This breaks down a certain area, for example, reading, into identifiable attitudes, skills and concepts. As each section is named and is easily recognisable, parents and ancillary staff can participate in observing and recording children's progress. However, ensure that they realise that children develop at different rates and while one may be able to draw a figure, another may make letter-type shapes.

However, the chart is limited as it provides little opportunity to describe individual styles of learning.

The profile

This is based on the observation of individual characteristics that emerge as children play. It contains details of what children actually do and say in specific situations. Such observation is useful because it focuses on the child as an individual rather than on specific skills. It highlights the child as a whole and may help identify the underlying factors that influence a child's achievement. It is useful for describing individual personal and

Alex D

Recently, Alex demonstrates an interest in music, creating a horn from
o rolled paper and playing Humpty Dumpty, holding a long brick as a guitar, singing
and spending considerable time listening to song and rhyme cassettes. Even
at the water tray, Alex shows fascination with the sound of water,
o splashing, blowing through tubes and dropping water at different rates on
surface, commenting, 'Its a drippy, drippy slish'.

social development, individual styles of learning and interests.

Schemata

Profiles enable staff to record a schema that is apparent in a child's play. As children investigate the world, they form schemata or frameworks, which are general ideas that they have formed and wish to explore further in a variety of settings. The idea that a child explores may be the idea of rotation or turning, and he investigates it by turning himself and objects. Certain objects that feature this aspect prominently will have a special fascination for the child at this time, for example, an axle with turning wheels or a screwdriver. Look out for other schemata, including transporting, covering, investigating spaces and the vertical. As you identify these, you will understand the reasons behind children's apparently random explorations of each area. Careful observation gives you insights into the ideas that children are developing as they repeat a certain set of behaviours using different materials and settings. Record your observations of what children do and say in a variety of settings.

Organising the records

The disadvantages of the profile lie in the fact that descriptions of schemata and other observations can be lengthy and diffuse. This can make it difficult for external agencies to glean the essential information. Record-keeping needs to be efficient and effective. You should not let it dominate daily activity to the extent that it stifles new initiatives, but rather it should be a productive element which contributes to the evaluation and planning of the curriculum. In this way, it may stimulate fresh directions.

Record-keeping stimulates discussion about individual children and activities, and this is as valuable as the records themselves. It is therefore important that as many people as possible contribute to them, including both staff and parents. This will give you several viewpoints on a child, each of which may reveal a different facet, and this will ensure that all staff are aware of points that need attention. For example, a child who is withdrawn may need to befriend one member of staff in the short term in order to overcome initial problems.

As the child's confidence increases, this may be reassessed and a new strategy adopted.

What do we record?

Observing children's play reaffirms that the foundations for early learning are very broad. Everything children do and say has its own significance. For some children, social development is a key factor. For others, encouragement to solve problems opens new areas of challenge and autonomy. The following are some guidelines for record-keeping.

• Always record a child's achievements.

• Include activities and experiences a child has undertaken, for example, using a computer.

• Include attitudes and skills, since motivation and physical competence are both fundamental to early learning.

• Take care before recording concepts or knowledge. Young children are still discovering the world and their concepts are still being formed and refined. A child may recognise a 'square' or 'red' in a card game or another limited context but not in a general context. For this reason, it is important to look at shades of red, for example, on a variety of objects and shapes.

• Include comments on a child's personal, social, physical and intellectual development.

• Include the implications for future practice.

Parents in partnership

A strong home-school liaison brings many benefits to all concerned, particularly the child. It bridges the gap between school and home, and builds the foundations for dialogue, understanding and mutual respect. Home provides an insight into the child in terms of both nurture and nature, since it is the place where relationships are first formed and where early learning takes place.

The nursery which offers a warm welcome to parents reaffirms the parents' role and ensures their continuing interest

in developing their child's full potential. We admit not only children but also their parents to school.

Parents are experts on their children and have access to a range of knowledge that lies outside the scope of the nursery or school, and yet influences the children's performance within it. Parents' talents and personalities can enrich the early years classroom. They represent the world of work and the community. Informed parents widen the horizons for young children's learning, providing a broad context for applying and developing individual skills. Parents sustain the continuity of interest and provide encouragement throughout the child's school career. This is mutually beneficial to the school and the child.

Welcoming parents

Even before a child enters school, there are many ways that you can welcome her and her parents.
• Visit the child and parent at home. Make sure that you arrange this in advance by letter or telephone.
• Make a 'Welcome' booklet explaining the routines of the school or nursery.

• Invite the parent and child to choose a book from the home library.
• Set up a toy library, offering a selection of toys that parents can borrow to use at home. These can often be combined with a mother and toddler club.
• Mother and toddler clubs can be invaluable if you have the facilities to set one up. These clubs usually meet once a week, and parents stay with their children, who are sometimes only a few weeks old. These clubs can be very valuable for parents who feel isolated, while children have the opportunity to get to know each other, the school or nursery and staff.

Flexible entry

Flexible starting arrangements ease the transition from home to school, helping both child and parent to be less worried about separation.
• Stagger the entry of new children to ensure that staff have adequate time to get to know each child and his parents.
• Encourage parents to stay with their children until they are settled.
• Make the session times flexible, for example, offer shorter sessions initially, until the child is settled and familiar with the routine.

Parent information

Most parents want to understand and become part of school life so that they can help their child. Explain the curricular basis of activities and offer helpful hints for encouraging play at home. You could try some of the following ideas.
• Make available brochures, pamphlets and leaflets on one theme, for example, water play, for parents to read and take away. Most parents are familiar with this style of information from supermarkets and clinics.
• Displays and class books featuring captioned photographs of children at play provide further information for parents.
• Make available information on the early years curriculum, and general information books, in a parent library.

• Put up posters describing new initiatives.
• Hang mobile posters over each area describing key concepts and skills that children acquire (see 'Informobiles', page 25).

Links between home and school

Once links between home and school have been formed, it is important to maintain them by ensuring that parents are given a positive and valuable role in their children's education. Parents sometimes need to be invited to share in developing their children's potential. To achieve this effectively, they need information and the opportunity to discuss developments with you. For example, you could try the following ideas.
• Establish shared reading schemes where parents and staff work together.
• Invite parents to observe and record the development of their child with you. Records provide a basis for discussion between staff and parents.
• Inform parents of the latest topic or subject for the investigation table so that

they can discuss this at home and contribute to the school collection.
• Invite parents to share their skills with the school. Seeing skills demonstrated is far more valuable to children than reading or being told about them. It also shows parents how much their skills are valued.
• Invite parents to participate in school activities, for example, baking and using a computer. This will make them feel part of the education process and will demonstrate to children that home and school have positive links. Home and school develop strong ties as parents become familiar with routines and staff, sharing activities with their child. Discussing school life at home will become more meaningful because parent and child are able to discuss it on an equal footing.

Ideas for parental involvement

The parent area

Make available an area where parents can have an informal chat with you and find out more about the school. As well as helping to make parents feel welcome, this would make a useful place for a parent and toddler club.

Try to provide a table, chairs and coffee-making facilities. It will also be useful to have a display board with information for parents, and another notice board for parents' own notices, perhaps advertising used clothes and toys. If possible, provide a small parent library stocked with books about young children.

Informobiles

Design a poster-style information sheet to hang over each area of the classroom. This should inform parents about what the children learn in each area. Make the posters as follows:
• Cut each piece of card into a relevant shape, for example, a bucket for the sand tray and a triangle or LEGO brick for the construction area.
• Devise a title and a list of key learning elements for each area, and write these on the shapes using bold lettering.
• Punch holes in the top of the card at each end, reinforcing the card on both sides with pieces of sticky tape.
• Thread string through the holes and suspend the cards from the ceiling.

A developmental diary

Make a 'diary' for each child, using a scrap book or large loose-leaf book with strong paper. Stick in a variety of items made or collected during the child's time at the nursery. These could include early mark-making and drawing, a hand print on entry and again at a later date, a friendship tree with playmates' names, stories and events which are important to the child, examples of cutting out, written examples of language use and paintings. Encourage parents to participate by bringing in photos and writing about the child's activities at home. Date the items to create a developmental record of the child.

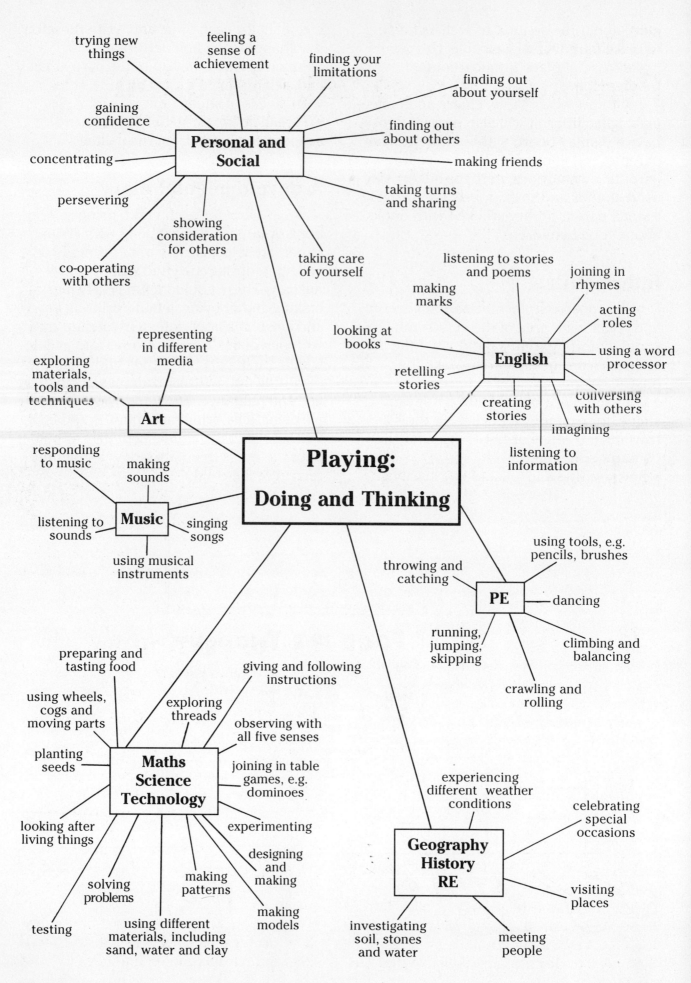

trying new
things

feeling a
sense of
achievement

finding your
limitations

finding out
about yourself

gaining
confidence

finding out
about others

concentrating

making friends

persevering

taking turns
and sharing

**Personal and
Social**

showing
consideration
for others

co-operating
with others

taking care
of yourself

**Playing:
Doing and Thinking**

representing
in different
media

exploring
materials,
tools and
techniques

Art

listening to stories
and poems

joining in
rhymes

making
marks

acting
roles

looking at
books

using a word
processor

retelling
stories

English

responding
to music

making
sounds

creating
stories

conversing
with others

listening to
sounds

Music

singing
songs

imagining

using musical
instruments

listening to
information

using tools, e.g.
pencils, brushes

throwing and
catching

PE

dancing

running,
jumping,
skipping

climbing and
balancing

crawling and
rolling

preparing and
tasting food

giving and following
instructions

using wheels,
cogs and
moving parts

exploring
threads

observing with
all five senses

planting
seeds

**Maths
Science
Technology**

joining in table
games, e.g.
dominoes

looking after
living things

experimenting

experiencing
different weather
conditions

celebrating
special
occasions

designing
and
making

solving
problems

making
patterns

**Geography
History
RE**

visiting
places

testing

using different
materials, including
sand, water and clay

making
models

investigating
soil, stones
and water

meeting
people

26

Chapter 2
Personal and social education

Personal and social education (PSE) permeates across and beyond the curriculum. It is not confined to subjects but is concerned with developing a broad and balanced outlook on life. PSE is a vital part of early years education as it influences a child's well-being and is concerned with her physical, social, emotional and moral welfare.

Most experiences raise moral issues. It is therefore important to agree on a moral framework with parents and governors. To assist with this, this chapter provides an outline of the main issues involved in PSE.

Many aspects of PSE appear daily in the life of the child and the school. The ethos and atmosphere of the environment is reflected in the way the child sees herself and others. In many ways, children learn PSE through their relationships with staff. Personal and social education is so important that it cannot be left to chance. Staff need to discuss it carefully so that the approach is consistent and understood by all. A sample recording chart is included on page 50.

Cross-curricular elements

The National Curriculum Council document *Curriculum Guidance 3: The Whole Curriculum* (NCC 1990) discusses the cross-curricular elements which make up personal and social education. The document divides these elements into three sections.
• Dimensions – equal opportunities, including considerations of gender, race and special needs, and multicultural education.
• Skills – communication, numeracy, study skills, problem-solving, personal and social skills and information technology.

• Themes – economic and industrial understanding, careers education and guidance, health education, education for citizenship, and environmental education.

This chapter follows the basic format outlined above, and considers the cross-curricular dimensions, skills and themes as they are relevant to early years education.

Dimensions

Equal opportunities

'Dimensions such as a commitment to providing equal opportunities for all pupils, and a recognition that preparation for life in a multicultural society is relevant to all pupils, should permeate every aspect of the curriculum.' (*Curriculum Guidance 3: The Whole Curriculum*, National Curriculum Council 1990.)

Children as young as three are aware of skin colour and may attribute different values to it. They are also aware of different sexes and may associate each sex with different roles and interests. These attitudes are not innate but learned, and may prevent children from achieving their maximum potential. Children need to be prepared for a multicultural society and for the changing roles of men and women, who both increasingly hold responsibilities at home and at work.

• When planning a policy of equal opportunities, you must consider the child's sense of her own ability and that of others, and the influence of your expectations of her achievement.•

One of the main goals of early years education has always been to build up children's self-esteem and self-respect by showing that they are valued members of the community. However, in considering gender and culture, you need to evaluate your own attitudes and expectations. These should not be limited by personal generalisations based on race, class or gender.

The early years environment should be multicultural and non-sexist, enabling all children, including those with special needs, to fulfil their potential. This requires a positive approach that will be evident in

the ethos and atmosphere of the school. Staff need to discuss the issues raised by equal opportunities and formulate a policy to adopt.

Gender

The term 'gender differences' refers to aspects of behaviour, goals, attitudes and expectations that are imparted by the way society views men and women, and not by individual capability. 'Sex differences' are biological ones. Traditionally, the roles of men and women have often varied according to their biological attributes, for example, women looked after children while men hunted for food. Many of the reasons behind this division of labour are no longer applicable in modern society and yet these ancient expectations still form part of the social fabric, and influence the lives of young children.

It is important to think about your expectations based on gender, because they may limit the activities and goals you provide for both girls and boys. Many children arrive at nursery with preconceptions about what they can do. These are often based on the type of toy they play with at home. They are drawn to familiar toys and continue their games, meeting others (usually of the same sex) with a similar taste in toys and activities. The cluster of girls in the home corner and

boys using LEGO is still a feature of many early years units. However, this does not have to be inevitable and unchangeable.

Why consider gender?

Gender bias may limit the activities chosen by girls and boys, as well as restricting their vision of their future role in society. It may prevent them from discovering their full range of abilities and talents and, in doing so, from achieving their true potential.

Role models

The following are some of the influences which form children's attitudes to gender differences.
• The work and roles of their parents.
• Their toys and clothes.
• Expectations about how they should play, for example, quietly or noisily, and what they are likely to be interested in, for example, going to a football match.
• Attitudes conveyed, for example, when they dirty their clothes, or in social interaction, for example, when children start fighting. Fighting may be thought acceptable for boys but not for girls.

Evaluating your attitudes

As gender attitudes are woven into the fabric of our lives, you need to honestly evaluate your own stance. One way of

Gender implications

You need to create an environment where boys and girls can participate fully in all areas of nursery experience, and in doing so achieve their potential. This requires a positive approach to planning the classroom environment.

• Consider the choice of equipment. An undefined wheeled vehicle may be chosen by boys and girls, whereas a police car is often attractive only to boys.

• Look at the arrangement of equipment. If you place an undefined building in the construction area it may become any building from a hotel to a hospital. Are there sufficient materials to make a hospital or home, as well as their related vehicles?

• Look at the pictures you display. These send messages about gender. For example, are girls as well as boys depicted playing with LEGO? Consider story and information books. Do these reinforce gender stereotypes, for example, by always showing girls playing with dolls? Are both women and men shown doing a wide range of jobs? Don't forget the pictures on jigsaws and computer graphics.

• Consider the messages given by the staff as role models. Do female staff use woodwork equipment as well as administer first aid?

• Think about your own expectations. Do you respond to children as 'boys' and 'girls' or as individuals? For example, when a child is hurt, your response may depend on the child's sex.

• Encourage children's participation in all areas and activities. Does one sex dominate one area or set of equipment? It may be that after a while, a certain area is associated with the same group of children, so that others do not try to play there. Try to let all the children have a free access. However, if the children always choose the same equipment, they will limit their experience. Be prepared to intervene to ensure that children have access to a variety of equipment.

• Do all areas appeal to both boys and girls? A role-play area, rather than a home

achieving this is to meet with colleagues to consider the following questions:

• Are certain areas of the nursery dominated by one sex?

• Do gender expectations influence your interaction with children? For example, do you always invite the boys to move large equipment and the girls to clean?

• Does the arrangement of materials invite only one sex to use them? For example, putting a garage and cars in the construction area may send out the message that this area is for boys.

• Do you interpret children's intentions and needs according to gender? For example, you may direct a child who has not chosen an activity to the home corner or construction area, depending on their sex.

• What messages do children receive from you as a role model, based on what you do and your attitudes to different activities? Do you prefer activities that reflect your gender and dismiss others without considering your ability to tackle them?

corner, encourages boys and girls to create their own roles in context. A home corner is often associated with girls.

• Try to counteract gender stereotypes. Make a positive effort to encourage girls' participation in construction and computer activities. Evaluate equipment, programs and access so that girls are given the opportunity to enjoy these activities. Boys may need encouragement to participate in caring activities. Create opportunities for them to play a leading role, for example, when a baby visits the nursery, ask a boy to help prepare the bath. Name a doll and encourage all the children to treat it as a baby. Let the children take turns in putting it to bed at the end of each session.

The role of staff

All staff should:
• evaluate their own attitudes and expectations based on gender;
• evaluate classroom equipment and areas to ensure they are not associated exclusively with any one gender;
• encourage children to participate in all areas;
• be aware of gender stereotypes and counter them with positive strategies.

Cultural diversity

When considering cultural diversity, there are two main aspects to bear in mind. Firstly, make sure that children from all cultures achieve their potential. Secondly, ensure that children are aware of the rich multicultural society in which we live.

Welcoming parents

Make sure that all children and their parents feel accepted and valued. Parents need to feel welcome. Invite them to participate in and become familiar with school activities, and encourage them to contribute to school life by sharing individual talents and interests.

It is important that parents can communicate with you, via a translator if necessary. They need to be informed in their own language about developments within the school. Equally, they need to inform you about their child. Some may be concerned about upholding cultural requirements, for example, those regarding food and clothes, and if this is the case, make a point of reassuring them about this.

Welcoming children

All children need to feel welcome in the early years classroom and to be included in the learning experiences. Make sure that they can identify with nursery activities and events, and let them see their culture reflected in school equipment and activities. They should be able to communicate with you, possibly through an interpreter in their family language. When possible, recruit staff who represent the ethnic composition of the school. Give the children the opportunity to acquire English as a second language. When you assess them, take care not to allow any cultural or linguistic bias to creep in. This is important if you are to help children

achieve their full potential. Finally, and possibly most importantly, make sure that the classroom is a non-racist environment.

A multicultural environment

Multicultural perspectives enrich the lives of all children. If you introduce children to the diversity of cultures, this will encourage them to respect each other (see pages 39 to 40 for further suggestions).

When you are planning a multicultural environment for your classroom, bear in mind the following questions.
• What are the predominant staff attitudes to and expectations of children from different races?
• Does your equipment reflect a multicultural society? Are there dolls reflecting different races?
• Do the pictures on posters, story-books and jigsaws reflect a multicultural society?
• Is your assessment of children culturally biased? For example, assessing children's ability to use cutlery may not be appropriate when fingers or chopsticks are used at home. Assessment of language needs special consideration, as some children may be bilingual. Take account of

the words they know in their family language rather than assessing them solely on their grasp of English. Being bilingual is a useful asset and its positive aspects need to be recognised and supported.

Prejudice

You need to honestly consider your own attitudes towards and expectations of children from different races. We all need to become aware of the different forms of prejudice. For example, biased attitudes may be passed on by implication in stories, even if they are not voiced openly. Check that characters of different races have a purposeful role in picture books and are not simply tokens. Ask yourself how much you know about other races and fill in the gaps as necessary.

Many young children play together regardless of race. However, some children imitate prejudiced attitudes they have heard or seen. Be careful how you react to prejudice from children. Over-reaction may result in separating the two parties even further, as one nurses a grievance and the other hurt pride. In responding to prejudice, consider how you can heal the gulf between the individuals.

Your role

• To ensure that all children and their parents feel accepted and valued.
• To ensure that all parents and children have the opportunity to speak to you.
• To provide a multicultural environment which enriches the lives of all children.
• To combat prejudice with positive strategies that heal divisions.
• To recognise the needs of ethnic minorities and provide the opportunities for children to achieve their potential, for example, by arranging language support.

Special needs

In the area of special needs, above all, you need to apply the principle and practice of working with children as individuals, that is, assessing their needs and planning to meet these so that each child can achieve his maximum potential.

When working with children with special needs, your role includes the following aspects:
• Assessing special needs. You need to observe children and keep records in order to assess effectively.
• Seeking specialist advice from the appropriate agency, for example, speech therapist or educational psychologist.
• Liaising with the relevant agency so that work with the child is maintained and supported.
• Guiding staff appointed to work with the child, to maintain progression and continuity.
• Liaising with parents to ensure that they are supported and informed of developments.
• Providing a warm, supportive atmosphere where children with special needs can participate without the fear of ridicule or prejudice.

Access to the full curriculum

With few exceptions, children with special needs are entitled to take part in the National Curriculum. According to the terms of the 1981 Education Act, they should be integrated as far as possible within mainstream schooling. Some children require special educational provision to enable them to do this. In these cases, parents are consulted and the child referred to the educational psychologist who usually makes the necessary arrangements.

When thinking about the environment you provide for children with special needs, consider the following factors:
• the building and arrangement of furniture, including access for wheelchairs and so on;
• staffing requirements, for example, when children require one-to-one care;
• the availability of resources and equipment that enable all children to participate, including children with physical or sensory difficulties;
• staff training;
• access to relevant specialists.
• the provision of any specific teaching the child requires;
• the co-ordination of the programme, including planning and liaison between school, home and specialist agencies.

Skills

There are certain skills that underlie all the different subject areas; these are the key skills essential to modern living. The skills are independent and can be nurtured in different contexts.

Communication

The ability to communicate is fundamental to learning and social development. A young child's need to communicate by speaking and listening is paramount. Provide activities that encourage children to explore communication through speech, mark-making, painting, drawing, music, movement, modelling and making charts.

On one occasion, some children in my nursery gathered round a collection of shells they found on a beach visit. They examined the shells carefully, turning each one to view it from a different perspective and looking at it through a magnifying glass. As they handled the shells, I wrote down their comments for captions on the investigation table. They discussed shape, saying 'this shell (a limpet) looks like a hat,' and 'this one (a whelk) has a big cave in it.' They described what the surface looked like, 'it's got pen lines' and how it felt, 'spiky', 'sandy' and 'prickly'. Placing a large shell to an ear, they described what they heard, 'I hear the wind whooo...'

Talking about things they see, feel and hear is often the first form of communication for children. It encourages them to think about their experiences and put them into words. They are comparing

and contrasting different features in order to name and express them to others. First the shells were described in words, and then the children chose to use other materials to represent different features of the shells. Some kneaded dough and clay into 'worms' that were wound into spirals, showing their fascination with shape; others mixed powder paint to match the colour on the shells; while others pressed shells into wet plaster and left these imprints to dry, noting the delicate raised patterns on the shell surfaces. The children were exploring different ways of communicating about the shells in their collection.

Numeracy

Children need to explore different types and uses of numeracy. They need access to meaningful everyday contexts where they can observe and participate at their own level. Provide activities that explore numeracy in the classroom, at home and in the wider community.

Daily life in the nursery or school provides many opportunities for children to use numeracy in context. Sorting equipment into the appropriate containers when tidying up and making collections of objects according to a named criterion, perhaps a shape or colour, are two activities that lay the foundations for numeracy. Matching one coat to a peg in the cloakroom and placing one straw in each milk carton are other daily tasks that children can undertake.

Baking involves estimating numbers and quantities and making lists with written numbers, for example, '4 apples'. When shopping, children are recognising written numbers on lists, counting the required number of objects and handling and counting money. The relevant terminology can also be introduced, as the buyer asks, 'How much does it cost?' and the shopkeeper says, 'Here's your change.' Baking involves counting and measuring quantity, weight, temperature and time. Sharing the end product means counting to ensure that there are enough pieces, or dividing a large cake or quiche into equal slices, which provides an early

introduction to fractions. Such activities introduce the functions and forms of numeracy in a meaningful way.

Study skills

Young children need to develop a thirst for learning and a curiosity about the world. Provide a stimulating and challenging environment where children are motivated to observe and explore. Self-initiated activities encourage children to concentrate and develop longer attention spans. This will provide a basis for study skills.

A visit from the fire service greatly stimulated the interest of children in my nursery. They watched as the fire officer demonstrated equipment including hoses, breathing apparatus and cutting gear. Children tried on helmets, climbed into the driving seat and spoke into the two-way radio. This stimulated play in many different areas of the nursery. In the role-play area, helmets, tubing, a steering wheel and luminous safety jackets provided the opportunity to explore 'being a fire-fighter'. Having seen the equipment used, children

created or improvised their own; a two-way radio was made with Brio Mec, a small block was placed on top of a longer one and used as 'a ladder', while the telephone was used to make emergency calls. Children listened avidly to stories and information books about the fire service, recalling what they had seen and showing interest in finding out more.

Problem-solving

You cannot presume that children will be willing to tackle problem-solving. They need to develop the confidence to try and the motivation to succeed by testing alternative strategies. Remind parents of the importance of letting children do tasks for themselves, from fastening their coat buttons to making models.

Provide open-ended situations and materials that encourage children to create and solve problems. Self-directed activity in the scrap materials area can offer scope for problem-solving when a variety of materials are available together with a selection of fasteners, for example, paper-clips, wool, paste and a stapler. Children may try using the same fastener on different materials, or different fasteners on the same material. They will be exploring types of materials and each discovery, regardless of whether or not it works, is a success in so far as it has brought them increased knowledge. Later, children will want to make a particular object, and their problem-solving will become focused on investigating alternatives to a specific problem. One child created a garden in a green shoe box. The sides were the fence, and flowers were cut from catalogues and greeting cards and pasted on the fence. Green material served as grass in the bottom of the box. However, a tree was required. First, the child chose a long, thin container because trees are 'high, higher than a fence,' but it toppled over. Searching in the materials, he found a tube and placed it in position, saying, 'Look. A tree. It's got a flat under it'.

The idea of trying alternatives is more useful than simply following adult directions. You can offer alternatives when the problem seems insurmountable and the child becomes frustrated. This gives children the support they need to achieve their goals. The young child needs space, materials and above all time to think and try out different ideas.

Personal and social skills

Young children need to develop personal and social skills in their interaction with others.

Give them opportunities to play alongside and with other children throughout the school. As they play with others, children learn about sharing and working together. Building large models or environments encourages children to discuss, plan and work together, stimulating imaginative play and social skills. Models built in co-operation with other children require a common purpose which is negotiated by the group. Imogen and Clare used large blocks to make a slide. Other children took turns on it. After a time, the girls decided to wedge another block underneath, making a bridge. Many

children strode over, chanting, 'Who's that trip-trapping over my bridge?' A troll was chosen and the game continued until the structure collapsed amidst the tears of Sam, the troll, and much speculation as to the cause.

Such play prepares children for their roles in the social world, and encourages them to explore their physical and social environment. Play gives children the freedom to determine the course of events and the level of interaction they undertake. As children make decisions among themselves and agree about how the materials are to be used, they are in fact making and subjecting themselves to rules that are far more complex and demanding than anything they can cope with in daily life. In play, children test their skills and capabilities to the limit.

Following rules or a social code of behaviour is the basis of social interaction. In the role-play area, children try out the roles of adults. At first, these roles are familiar and predictable: 'You be the mummy and I'll be the little girl.' In these roles they repeat familiar 'scripts' that they associate with the characters, for example, 'Put on your coat. We're going to the shop.' Later, children create complex and imaginative sequences that draw on many aspects of their experience and feelings. In playing with others, children are accumulating a wealth of skills, confidence and experience that is useful in daily interactions with others.

Information technology

Information technology (IT) deals with the storage, processing and transmission of information and its use in controlling

machines. Most young children are already familiar with IT in the form of television and computers. Give the children opportunities to explore IT in a meaningful and relevant way. Children need to enjoy and be confident in their approach to modern technology.

Computer toys with rechargeable batteries are a useful introduction to control technology. These have simple systems of signs and buttons that are user-friendly for young children. They enjoy exploring the toy's potential for movement and start to associate the sign and the movement. Choose a computer toy that may easily be converted into a vehicle, person or animal and used alongside other equipment.

A piece of fur with two dark felt-tip eyes was stuck on to the computer toy to indicate that it was a dog. 'It's my Bonnie,' declared one child. A cardboard box served as a kennel and a carton for a dog bowl. When the children were familiar with the possible moves that 'Bonnie' could make, we set them challenges. Bonnie was set down in a far corner and the children were told that Bonnie was lost and needed help to find the way back to her kennel. Children worked together trying out moves that would take Bonnie home. Each move the hungry Bonnie made that took her further away from her dinner caused great consternation. Avoiding shelf units and table legs was a further challenge because of the possible injuries and distress that Bonnie might suffer. In this way technology became another toy for children to explore and discover its potential.

Themes

Citizenship

Early years education introduces children to living in the wider community. Here, children are encouraged to participate, contribute and take responsibility for themselves. Children are citizens at school or nursery, at home and in the wider

community, and an awareness of citizenship encompasses all three areas.

School or nursery

The school community

It is important that a child's first step into the school or nursery community is a calm and secure transition; it may influence his whole outlook on education. Home/school liaison ensures that children see the home and school as environments that complement each other rather than as separate entities each with its own set of rules.

In the early years classroom, children learn to trust other adults and to get to know other children. They learn that there are a few simple rules, for example, no running inside the school.

Here are some ideas for encouraging children to take responsibility for themselves.

• Encourage children to initiate, plan, follow through and tidy up after their activities.
• Check that the position of equipment encourages children to see to their own needs. Are coat pegs accessible? Are sinks, toilets and towels at child height? Are aprons easy to slip over their heads and to fasten?

A pluralist environment

Create a multicultural environment within the school so that all children can be enriched by cultures other than their own. Encourage children to participate in activities and events that have their origins in many cultures. These enjoyable experiences provide the foundation for mutual respect. You might like to try some of the following ideas.
• Read stories about children from many cultures.
• Read traditional stories from different

cultures, for example, the Caribbean stories about Anansi the spider man.
• Celebrate events from different cultures, for example, the Chinese New Year.
• Let the children sample food from different cultures.

A sense of responsibility

As members of the nursery or school, children should be encouraged to become independent by seeing to their own needs and choosing activities. Children should learn to be responsible for looking after and tidying away equipment. Encourage them to consider the needs of others and to take turns with equipment.

There are various ways of encouraging children to co-operate with you and with each other.
• Provide picture labels and silhouettes to assist children to put away equipment.
• Make sure that the children know how many can play effectively in any one area. Place the appropriate number of aprons in the paint area, for example, as an indication. As an alternative, each child can hang his picture tag on one of a limited number of pegs in the area where the activity is taking place.

Democracy in action

Making choices is the basis of democracy. Give the children choices in all areas of the curriculum so that they become familiar and confident in decision-making. For example:
• provide a choice of materials for model-making;
• let the children choose from a variety of ingredients to taste;
• at times, offer children a choice of stories to be read to the whole group.

The citizen and the law

The early years classroom has a few simple rules to ensure the safety of everyone. Children simultaneously learn these rules and the reason for them. They also learn

TASTING TABLE

40

the consequences of breaking the rules, for example, if they deliberately break equipment, it will no longer be available.

Here are a few ideas for helping children to understand the concept of rules.
• Agree a few simple but necessary rules with your colleagues and apply them consistently.
• Agree on a course of action for children who do not abide by the rules, for example, not allowing the child to play in the area where she misbehaved and taking her to an area such as the clay table, where damage is less likely and where she can work out her individual frustrations.
• Always explain to the child why her behaviour is unacceptable and how it can be improved.
• Listen to the child to ensure that, as far as possible, justice is done and seen to be done.

The family

Children enjoy meeting family members, for example, babies and grandparents. There are plenty of other ideas you can use to help children develop an awareness of family relationships.
• Make a photo montage to show how parents look after their children, for example, preparing food, buying clothes and toys.
• Invite a baby into the classroom and let the children watch as its parent bathes, feeds and clothes it.
• Encourage children to talk about jobs they can do at home, for example, tidying away toys and clearing the table.

Society

Using leisure time

There are several ways of helping children make full use of the leisure facilities on offer locally.
• Inform parents of local activities that children may enjoy, for example, swimming and gym sessions. Post leaflets on the parents' noticeboard with details of places and times.
• Take children to visit the library.

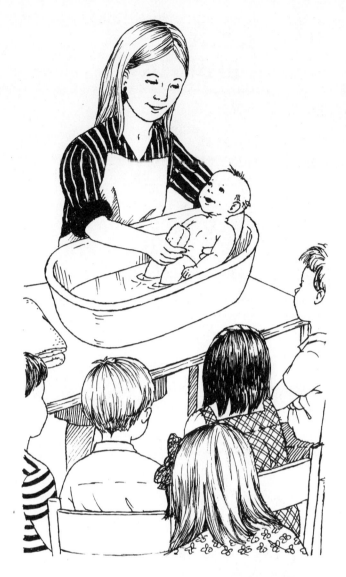

• Local museums and exhibitions can often be interesting, but many have stands and displays which are too high for children to see, so check this before you visit.
• Invite parents to contribute photos of their child enjoying a local leisure pursuit and use the photos as a focus for discussion.

Public services

Most children have regular contact with many public services, including the dentist, doctor and clinic. Many of these will allow their staff to come into the school to meet the children and talk about their role in the community. Meeting people who work for the ambulance service and police and finding out what they they do also helps to allay any fears the children may have.

41

Explore the theme of 'people who help us' through role-play. For example, you could:
• make an ambulance or fire-engine using large boxes so that children can explore how these vehicles are used;
• set up a library where children can choose, sort and stamp books.

Your role

Your role in helping a young child become a responsible citizen includes helping him to develop the following qualities:
• self-esteem and self-reliance;
• self-control and self-discipline;
• respect and consideration for others;
• an interest in the world and the things in it, both natural and man-made;
• a sense of fairness;
• a willingness to help others;
• a sense of pride in and responsibility for the school;
• a positive attitude to school and learning.

Health education

'Standards, attitudes and patterns of behaviour can convey powerful messages and their significance is often underestimated. Lessons which promote courtesy, concern, respect and acceptance of responsibility for self and others will be more effective if these qualities are valued consistently in every aspect of school life.' (*Curriculum Guidance 5: Health Education*, National Curriculum Council 1990.)

Health education in the early years is about the development of the whole child. You need to make this part of a planned policy and yet you must also put across the essential messages through your relationships with children and in the general atmosphere of the classroom. Children need a secure environment where they can develop a positive self-image and learn about themselves and others. Your policy on health education should emphasise:
• the children's emotional well-being, self-esteem and self-confidence;
• their social confidence and self-discipline in playing with others;
• their physical well-being, knowledge about their bodies and ability to take care of themselves;
• links with local health services and parents.

Environmental aspects of health education

Establish and maintain a warm, friendly, comfortable and secure environment, where the children will recognise the familiar faces of the staff and where the daily routine is familiar and consistent.

Individuals influence an environment. Staff need to set good examples for the children, for example, they should speak calmly and quietly and demonstrate tidy habits. Encourage children to look after equipment and books. Invite them to help mend any broken equipment and clear up any untidy corners.

Emphasise any environmental aspects of health in context. For example, point out the importance of hygiene when preparing food for others to taste.

Psychological aspects

Before children can value themselves, they need to be valued by others. You can demonstrate this visibly by giving them attention and understanding. The home also contributes to the child's self-image. It is important to accept and value both the child and his parents. Welcome parents to the school so that children have the security of a close relationship between home and school. Close liaisons enable parents to continue to play an important role in their child's education. Invite parents to help in the classroom to ensure that children benefit from mutual activities that break down unnatural barriers between home and school.

Young children often demonstrate sudden and extreme emotions. These emotions of anger, excitement or unhappiness seem to take them over and they often frighten themselves and others with their intensity. In these situations, you must respond to the child rather than react to the emotion. Explain the emotion to the child, for example, saying 'You're feeling cross because...'. A calm, positive and supportive approach will help children to understand their emotions and learn self-control.

This role also applies to unacceptable behaviour. Children need to understand why it is unacceptable, for example, because it hurts others, and they must be offered acceptable alternative ways of

behaving. Again, this will help them develop self-control and self-discipline and enable them to co-operate with others.

Encourage children to take turns and share. Many board games and pieces of equipment, for example, the climbing frame, depend on this to be fully enjoyed.

Personal hygiene

Personal hygiene routines, such as washing hands after going to the toilet and before handling food, should be emphasised as the situation arises. Encourage these routines consistently and explain why they should be done. The school nurse and dentist are usually willing to talk to children and parents about health and hygiene. Post leaflets on the parents' noticeboard about personal hygiene to encourage these routines at home. Invite children to help with routines that keep the school clean, for example, washing equipment and dressing up clothes.

Here are some more ideas for promoting hygiene:
• Sing songs about personal hygiene, for example, 'Here we go round the mulberry bush'.
• Discuss information books containing photos of children washing and brushing their teeth and hair.
• Read stories, for example, *Postman Pat's sore tooth* by John Cunliffe (Hippo) and use these as a basis for discussing children's experiences.

Safety

Inform children of the dangers of different environments, in particular roads, water and the home. RoSPA (The Royal Society for the Prevention of Accidents) send people into schools to talk about road safety.

Safety in the school can be a good starting point for considering different aspects of safety. For example, using wheeled toys may lead to a discussion on road safety; using the oven may bring up the topic of safety in the home and using electrical equipment may lead to a discussion about the potential dangers of electricity.

Buy a wide variety of foods including fruit, vegetables and milk products, and let the children taste them and give their verdict. As they do so, discuss why certain foods are better for us and why we need to eat.

Put good nutrition into practice in the food area by not making too many sweet dishes. Try using wholemeal flour instead of white.

Health-related exercise

Provide regular interesting and challenging physical play so that children enjoy exercise and see it as part of their lives. Give them a chance to experience movement to music, ring games and other forms of indoor exercise. Provide an open space for running, jumping and skipping, and if possible, supply equipment for the children to climb, slide down and crawl through.

Family life education

Ask the children to consider their own family and its members. Approach this in a sensitive way so that all children feel that their family is valued.
• Talk about ways in which different family members look after the children.
• Encourage children to think about how they can contribute to family life.
• Encourage them to bring in photos, garments and memorabilia from weddings and other family occasions.
• Invite children to bring in photos of themselves as babies and toddlers.
• Provide children with the opportunity to take care of animals, under supervision.

Sex education

Many young children have new sisters and brothers during their time in the early years unit. A new baby can present the opportunity to discuss the birth and care of babies in a loving context. Many pregnant mums are willing for you to follow the later stages of their pregnancy and will then bring the new baby to meet the children. Invite the father, too. Many children are already aware that their new baby is 'growing in mummy's big tummy' and some

Use a range of stories, songs and rhymes as a way of introducing safety. For example, 'Polly put the kettle on' is a focus for discussing electricity and hot water. You could make up an additional verse that reinforces these ideas, for example:

Never touch the kettle,
Never touch the kettle,
Never touch the kettle,
It's getting very hot.

Place leaflets about safety on the parents' noticeboard. These could include using car seat belts, safe parking outside the school gates, and safety at home.

Substance use and misuse

Warn children not to eat or drink anything without first asking a responsible adult. Draw their attention to the dangers of berries, medicines and cleaning agents.

Food and nutrition

Meal times and cookery sessions provide ideal opportunities for letting the children taste foods from different cultures. Invite parents to bring in dishes eaten at home.

even paint pictures featuring the small baby inside the mother. Breast feeding and nappy changing are a part of everyday life for many young children.

Make sure that young children know that they have rights over their own body. They should be able to talk to you about any event that makes them unhappy or uncomfortable. Be alert for signs of sexual or physical abuse and refer to LEA guidelines.

Environmental education

The aim of environmental education is to encourage an awareness of the world around us and to nurture a sense of respect and responsibility for it.

Environmental education has three inter-related components.

Education about the environment

This includes knowledge about climate, soil, rocks, water, plants and animals. Children learn about these by first-hand experience. For example, make collections of stones from the garden or pebbles from the seashore and ask children to suggest how they differ and why.

Children should also learn about the manufactured environment – people and communities, energy, buildings, industry and waste. Start by looking at the school as a community where people have different functions. Look at the buildings and grounds and how they are used. Look at the sources of energy used and what happens to waste materials. Discuss industries in which parents work or which are of particular interest, and consider the products they make or the services they provide. (See Chapter 6 for more information about these topics.)

Education for the environment

This encourages values and attitudes that develop a positive approach to environmental affairs. Children who appreciate both natural and man-made creations are likely to develop a caring attitude.

Involve children in looking at and looking after the school environment. Let them observe living things outside the classroom and plant seeds and shrubs. They can also observe the equipment; discuss the materials they are made from and how they are made. Encourage children to look after equipment carefully.

Education in and through the environment

This involves first-hand experience of the environment in order to develop personal attitudes towards environmental issues. Planting bulbs and flowers in the school grounds may make children aware of why they should not leave litter.

Walk around the school grounds, emphasising different features each time:
• sounds we can hear;
• things we can smell;
• textures we can feel.

Careers education and guidance

'During the pre-school years, children acquire an awareness of work in the home and their immediate neighbourhood. Their impressions are formed by their parents, other adults whom they see working and media influences.' (*Curriculum Guidance 6: Careers Education and Guidance*, National Curriculum Council 1990.)

Children learn about the world of work from the people they meet, and act out roles as they play. Stories and information books also introduce children to working life. Make sure that you counter stereotypes of gender or race that may restrict young children's aspirations. Choose books and display materials that feature, for example, female pilots. Invite male nurses and female doctors to school to talk about their work.

Although it is too early to ask children what they would like to be when they grow up, you can help the children to get to know themselves and introduce them to the world of work.

Forming an impression about themselves

In the early years classroom, children are offered new experiences and challenges that allow them to discover and practise new skills. Help them to enjoy doing this and to feel a sense of personal achievement so that they can face the world with confidence.

Identifying and describing jobs

Children need to meet adults who will describe or demonstrate their work. Invite the following people in to talk about their work and to bring any relevant items of equipment:
• school staff, for example, the cleaner, cook and gardener;

• people who visit the school in the course of their work, for example, people who deliver goods, letters or milk;
• parents;
• people who work in public services, for example, the police and fire service.

Exploring adult work roles

Listen with the children to stories about different jobs and give them the opportunity to act out these roles in imaginative play. Set up a role play area as a café, a hairdresser's or a hospital.

Economic and industrial understanding

'Education for economic and industrial understanding... explores economic aspects of [pupils'] present lives. It prepares them for future economic roles: as producers, consumers and citizens in a democracy.' (*Curriculum Guidance 4: Education for Economic and Industrial Understanding*, National Curriculum Council 1990.)

Many activities for promoting economic awareness can be built on the children's previous experience. Explore these experiences further and clarify them. Give the children the opportunity to participate in real and imaginative activities. For example, you can do some real shopping for the food area and set up different types of shop in the role-play area. You could try the following activities to bring out different aspects of economic awareness.

Shopping

Help children to make decisions about what they need to buy, for example, by reading out a recipe and writing out a list of ingredients. Help them to make choices, perhaps deciding which ingredients to choose when there is an option, for example, when making a pizza topping or fruit salad.

Help the children to understand our basic needs. Discuss why we need food. In cold weather, discuss why we wear warm clothes before setting out to the shop.

Look at our role as consumers. On the way to the supermarket, look at different shops and services, for example, the library and post office.

In the shop, look at the whole business of buying and selling. Invite the children to select the goods required and pay for them. Meet the shop assistant and watch as he fills the shelves and calculates how much customers need to pay.

Cooking

Help the children to understand how things are produced. When tasting or baking, ask the children to look at different foods. For example, show them some tomato purée, and discuss how this is made from tomatoes. In the food area, show children how some everyday items are made, for example, bread, soup and cakes.

Read the recipe before you start cooking, and describe all the different jobs that need doing and how they are done, for example, sieving flour, measuring ingredients, stirring or whisking and dividing into containers. Remind children of when they went shopping and of the tasks that still remain, including the washing up.

Gather all the equipment required for preparing the food. Name the tools and describe how they are used. Give children the opportunity to use them under your supervision.

Go into business!

Set up a mini-enterprise where children bake cakes or pot out seedlings to sell. Use the money to buy a new piece of equipment. Cut out pictures of three items that the money the children have raised could buy. Let them each indicate with a sticker or mark which one they prefer and order the item that most children request. Show children the catalogue and invite them to watch as you fill in the order form and later post it.

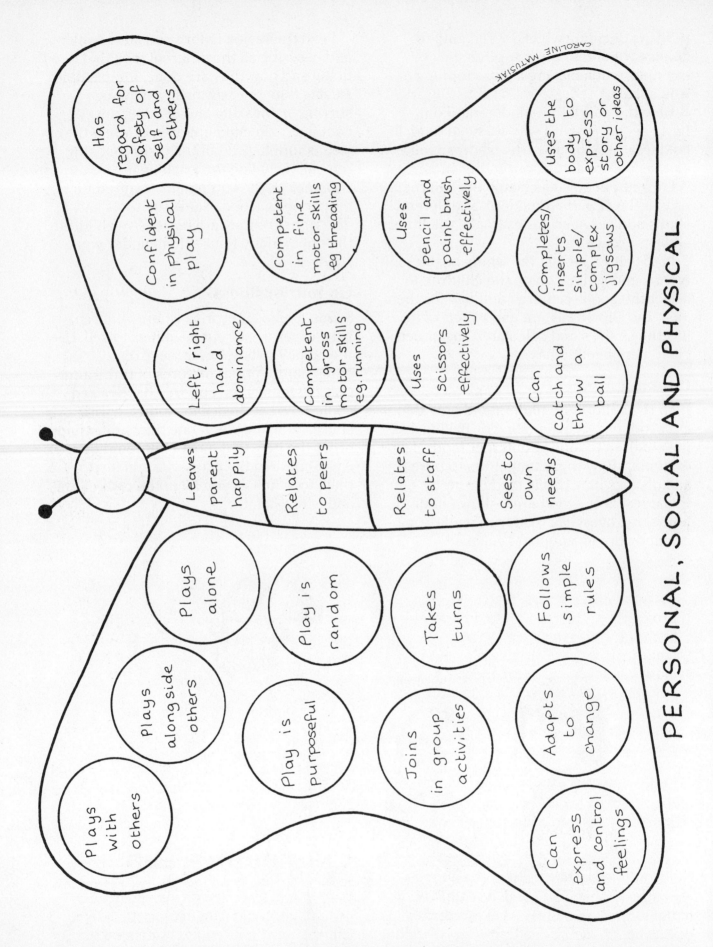

CAROLINE MATUSIAK

Has regard for safety of self and others

Confident in physical play

Competent in fine motor skills eg threading

Uses pencil and paint brush effectively

Uses the body to express story or other ideas

Completes/inserts simple/complex jigsaws

Left/right hand dominance

Competent in gross motor skills eg. running

Uses scissors effectively

Can catch and throw a ball

Leaves parent happily

Relates to peers

Relates to staff

Sees to own needs

Plays alone

Play is random

Takes turns

Follows simple rules

Plays alongside others

Play is purposeful

Joins in group activities

Adapts to change

Plays with others

Can express and control feelings

PERSONAL, SOCIAL AND PHYSICAL

Chapter 3
English

'Listening, speaking, reading and writing are fundamentally important activities in young children's learning. Good provision promotes ideas and responses from the children which they may communicate in a variety of ways but the modes of language claim special attention.' (Her Majesty's Inspectorate, *Aspects of Primary Education: The Education of Children under Five,* HMSO 1989.)

Children need to experience language and literacy to help them become good readers and writers. You and the children can initiate activities where language and literacy are used for different purposes.

It is important to accept and value the accent or mother tongue of *all* the children in the class. If you provide an interesting environment and interesting conversation this will help prompt children to talk. Encourage early reading and writing skills by providing suitable materials and play contexts. Stories provide a pleasurable way of introducing children to books and print. They are also a way of getting parents involved. Children need to share books and understand the uses of print. Let them experiment with its forms and create their own meanings.

This chapter will consider the importance of language in the early years in general terms, and then go on to discuss the areas of speaking and listening, reading and writing in more detail. There is also a sample recording chart on page 89.

Communication

We communicate and exchange ideas primarily through language, both spoken and written. Children are motivated to learn to speak, write and read because these are useful skills.

Uses of language

Person to person

Language is our means of socialising with each other during the course of the day. Speech, in particular, allows us to interact on a personal level. Our words, tone and gesture reflect our emotional state, whether it is friendly or aggressive. Written signs send messages in the same way, for example, 'Do not disturb' and 'Welcome'.

Communicating ideas

One way of learning is through expressing ideas and receiving them from other people. We need to listen to each other, ask questions, read instructions and seek out other sources of information.

Learning about the world

Putting our own newly-perceived ideas into words is an important part of learning. The ability to name and describe objects and ideas allows us to talk about these things out of context. In this way, we can compare and contrast ideas so that we will eventually form new concepts. For example, the ability to describe a circle means that when we see a different shape, we realise it is not a circle. This can provide the basis for further concepts about shapes, perhaps leading to the recognition of squares, triangles and so on.

Whole language

Speaking, listening, reading and writing are closely interrelated in our use of language. Written language and speech differ in form, but both are rooted in social interaction. The family is the child's first source of language and literacy, where he learns simultaneously about the purpose and the meaning of spoken and written language. He watches as his parents discuss, read and fill in forms. Speaking, listening, reading and writing are interdependent parts of the social processes of family life.

It is important that you maintain this whole language approach in the early years classroom. To achieve this, you must make the child's encounters with spoken and written language meaningful. Work on tasks together with children, each sharing the same goal. In this way, both of you can explain and negotiate your intentions and ideas. Such a partnership will provide the basis for integrating speaking and listening, reading and writing.

There are various ways of maintaining the whole language approach. Make sure that reading and writing materials are available in many parts of the nursery or classroom. For example, encourage the

children to read and write shopping lists in the class shop. When you or the children tell stories, write them down in a book for the children to read later.

An environment for language and literacy

Make the classroom a place where language and literacy are prominent and useful. Consider each area in turn and ask the following questions:
• Do the layout and equipment encourage children to talk?
• Is there space for children to work together?
• Is there enough equipment to share?
• Is the material stimulating and open-ended so that it invites discussion and decisions?
• Are there opportunities for the children to listen to each other, to staff and to recorded cassettes?
• Are there plenty of relevant reading materials in the form of signs, labels, story-books and information books?
• Are writing materials freely available, including pencils, pads and clipboards?

Apprenticeship for language

Spoken and written language have forms and conventions that have to be learned in order to use them properly. An adult or older child introduces language to the young child at home, in a way that she will understand. As the adult knows the child, he will be able to interpret what she is trying to say or write in reply. Even the babble of a baby means something to the parent, who responds by talking, perhaps about a toy the baby is playing with. The adult assumes that the child is trying to communicate something that is meaningful. The child is encouraged to continue to make sense of speech and print.

You can continue this apprenticeship approach to language in the early years classroom. For example, you can comment on a child's drawing, 'What a lovely picture. Tell me about it'. You can respond positively towards it, even if you cannot make out what it is. By doing so, you encourage the child to demonstrate her knowledge about spoken and written language.

At home, adults offer a model of language and literacy in use. A child listens and observes as his parent chats with friends, or fills in cheques and allowance books. On occasions, the child will be invited to participate, perhaps drawing kisses on grandma's card or discussing the clothes he is going to wear. The adult adapts his speech so that the child understands, or suggests written contributions that a child can make. For instance, the child can be invited to write his name at the bottom of a card. Children attempting to say something more difficult will be offered adult help, perhaps by giving them time or suggesting possible phrases. Your role is to emulate these aspects of parental support. You can do this in several ways:

• Create an environment where language and literacy has an essential and evident place.
• Encourage children to demonstrate their language and literacy skills by helping them to join in conversations and participate in reading and writing for different purposes.
• Help children to use language and literacy effectively, by taking over the parts they cannot do. In this way, they can achieve their goal, for example, writing a letter to a sick relative.
• Invite children's participation in language and literacy, for example, in discussing the siting of a piece of equipment or writing labels for display.
• Demonstrate how language and literacy is used. Employ talking, writing and reading to achieve a class or personal goal.
• Provide activities and materials that are meaningful and that motivate children to talk, read and write.

Speaking and listening

Spoken language has a central role in the social, intellectual and emotional development of the young child. Being able to talk enables children to share, plan and co-operate with others. Knowing that their contributions are valued will give them the confidence and security to talk with others.

Children need someone to talk with, either adults or other children. They also need something to talk about. This should not be difficult to find in an interesting and challenging play environment. Give them time to express their ideas, and listen carefully to what they are saying.

The central role of language

Through speaking and listening, children's social awareness, imagination and intellect will all develop and grow.

Social skills

Conversation in its true sense depends on the development of social skills. It means taking turns, listening and responding to others. At first, language is used as a means of demarcation ('That's mine'), but later children use language as a means of bargaining and ensuring that their turn will come, and this may involve asking you to intervene for fair play. A child's familiarity with language improves his social skills, since he no longer needs to rely on physical means, that is, pushing and snatching, to communicate his needs. Polite terms such as 'hello', 'thank you' and 'please' are rarely appreciated by young children as they do not see them as a necessary part of their dialogue, which is limited to practical requests. How often children use these terms is influenced by their home, but you can encourage children to use polite phrases, as they form part of our social interaction.

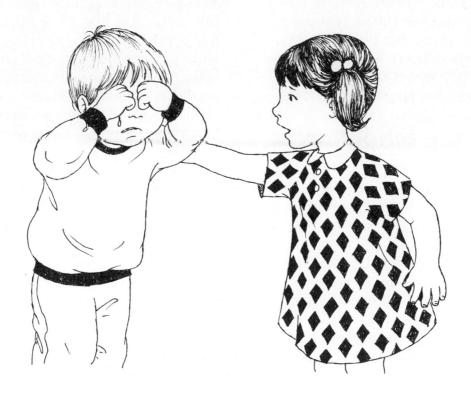

Imaginative development

Being able to express their fears, dreams and feelings helps children to become emotionally stable. Children gradually come to terms with their feelings as they show their emotions and are consoled by those around them. In recognising their own feelings, they eventually realise the need to be considerate towards others.

Young children can offer support to their unhappy peers, perhaps saying, 'It will all be better soon'. This is the root of empathy, an essential ingredient of story-telling and imaginative writing. Responding to stories depends upon an ability to identify with the feelings and situation of the story's characters, and being able to put yourself in 'someone else's shoes'. When they can do this, children are able to create their own characters in role-play, becoming someone else, imitating actions, words and attitudes.

Intellectual development

To a large degree, a child's ability to talk influences her thinking. For example, it determines her capacity for naming and describing objects, people, events and activities. By naming or labelling things, for example, a dog, children show that they can recognise their characteristics, that is, an animal with four legs and a tail. This is why a young child just starting to talk may call all animals with four legs and a tail 'dog'. Later, this will be refined as a new criterion, for example, barking, is applied. This limits the concept of 'dog' and introduces the possibility of other terms to describe animals that do not bark, for example, 'cat' and 'mouse'.

When a child encounters something new, she will describe it in words she already knows, for example, she may call a bear a 'dog'. An adult encourages her to think carefully about both animals by describing the features that differentiate bears and dogs, and in this way the child acquires a new concept. The words need to be used and applied in a variety of situations as there are so many different types of dogs and bears. Later, children appreciate more general concepts, for example, the idea of animals in general, and can apply generic terms. This process of recognition continues throughout the early years as children talk about what they are seeing, doing and experiencing. The more a child experiences and communicates with an adult, the more her language will develop.

Talk in the school or nursery

Planning for talk

Consider the early years classroom and ask yourself the following questions.
• Are there sufficient opportunities for children to work together? For example, large bricks, sturdy floor jigsaws and train tracks encourage children to plan and talk together.

• Do you actively encourage children to talk with each other? The nursery will be noisy, but a glance around the room will ensure that children are talking about their tasks. Check the noise level to ensure that no child needs to shout to be heard. Soft furnishings and fabrics are extremely useful in early years units to ensure that sound is absorbed.
• Is there a range of experiences and activities which stimulate children to talk? Introduce new objects, people, animals and places to widen children's experience and thereby increase their vocabulary.
• Do you make the most of parents and others willing to help? Invite parents, grandparents and student teachers to talk with the children as they play.

Language across the curriculum

Children need the opportunity to experience and discuss activities relating to all areas of the curriculum. This is stated in the National Curriculum documents. A child needs to acquire the language and concepts that are at the heart of each subject area. This enables the child to compare and contrast experiences and attributes. Language is the key that unlocks the doors to further learning and opens the way to higher order skills such as hypothesising, problem-solving and decision-making. These in turn provide the foundations for science, maths and technology.

Stages of language development

Each child acquires language at his own pace and in his own way. Some children say nothing and then speak suddenly in sentences, whilst for others learning to talk is a gradual progression. This does not depend on age, but on how much a child is exposed to and involved with language, that is, how much others talk with him. One child in my nursery had been left for long periods on her own in her bedroom. On entry, she did not even know her own name. She was given an intensive language programme. As a result, she progressed through all the stages, babbling, parroting and labelling but at a much quicker rate. Each stage is equally important, as it lays the foundation for the next.

Babbling

Babies babble the sounds that form all languages. As a baby hears and becomes accustomed to his own language, he starts to babble the sounds of his own language. French babies babble in French while American babies babble in American.

Imitating

Toddlers imitate or 'parrot' single words or phrases. These are usually words that they hear a lot in their family routine, for example, 'daddy', or 'dinner'. However, children do not just imitate, as they apply words they know to different contexts, for example 'daddy' may denote 'man', much to the amusement and embarrassment of parents! Toddlers often imitate the sounds made by a vehicle or animal and give that as the object's name, for example, 'quack, quack' for duck.

Labelling

Later, two words are combined to make a phrase that names a person or object and describes what it does. A child applies these phrases to many situations, and they can mean different things in each situation. 'Dindin gone', may mean 'I've finished my dinner', 'My dinner has fallen on the floor' or 'The dog has eaten my dinner.' An adult with the child will understand the real meaning and respond accordingly, 'Oh no, the dog has eaten your dinner.' In this way the child has her statement repeated in the accepted form which will help her in the future.

Simple sentences

Gradually children build up the experience and vocabulary to use simple sentences to express their needs, for example, 'Me wants dinner.' Parents who talk with children about daily events and describe what they

are seeing and doing give their children further possibilities for language and a model to copy. For example, when out on a walk, the parent might say, 'Look at that bird. It's got brown wings and a red chest. It's called a robin.'

Complex sentences

Some young children can use language for a variety of purposes, perhaps to reason why rain falls in stripes down the window pane or to describe in detail and at length a recent outing to the zoo. These children need time to express their ideas fully. You should support them and show your interest intermittently, saying 'Really', or 'And what happened next?'

What school can learn from home

At home, parents respond not just to a child's words but to what she intends. Every utterance, from babbling onwards, is seen as meaningful. During the course of family life, children initiate most conversations. Parents and children have conversations, that is, each takes turns. The adult can sustain a child's contribution by showing interest, and by following up a child's ideas, saying perhaps, 'And what did it look like?', or encouraging a child's efforts by saying 'Mmm', which means, 'Carry on talking. I'm listening.' Such conversations reflect the child's interests and thinking. They therefore encourage the child to talk at greater length and use more complex language structures.

In the early years classroom, teachers often dominate and direct a child's use of language. In the past, teachers would ask questions, for example, 'What colour is that?' or 'What is this called?' These closed questions require only a one-word answer. They do not encourage a child to develop and use complex language structures and employ higher order thinking skills. However, open questions, such as 'How can we make your boat move?' require children to consider alternatives, make suggestions and predict possible outcomes. Direct questions have a role in everyday social interaction, but ensure that they are kept to a minimum. Encourage conversation which makes more demands on a child's social and language skills.

Conversations

Act as an interested parent by listening to the child, sustaining her efforts and contributing to the conversation. Ask yourself the following questions:

• Do you give children the opportunity to start the conversation?
• Do you encourage children to talk? Listen to children and make an appropriate contribution, as you would to a friend. 'Oh, I've got a kitten. He's...'. Conversations should not be just a monologue by the child, but a two-way dialogue between adult and child.
• Do you really listen to what the child is saying? Real interest will show when you make an appropriate response not just to her words but also to her meaning, which will encourage the child to continue.
• Do you help to sustain the child's efforts to put his experience into words? This is termed 'scaffolding', in other words, supporting a child as he seeks to express himself.
• Are you patient when a child hesitates? Give him time before you offer words which may put him off the track.
• Do you show an interest in a lengthy dialogue by saying, 'Mmm,' and making other sustaining noises?
• Do you encourage children to talk further by asking relevant open questions, such as 'And what happened next?'
• Do you try to create time to listen to children? You need to recognise language development as a priority and organise your time accordingly.

Teacher talk

Consider the nature of teacher talk. How much is to do with management, for example, 'Hang your coats up' or 'Tidy up these bricks'? There may also be a large number of exclamations such as, 'Well done, Matthew'. Neither of these demand a spoken response from the children, although they may demand a physical one. If a large proportion of the things you say are to do with management rather than conversation, perhaps you could review how you run the class or change the timetable to keep transitions from one activity to another to a minimum. Change-overs with large groups of children often require a great deal of management talk. For this reason, make the routine

predictable and familiar to the children so that they can proceed as independently as possible.

Language for different purposes

Offer the children examples of language structures and use. You need to put into words what children are doing, seeing, hearing and feeling, for example, 'I see you are folding the paper'. Read texts with a variety of language structures, for example, poetry, rhymes, stories and non-fiction. Playing games encourages children to give and follow instructions.

Encourage children to use language for different purposes:
• to recall past events;
• to predict what may happen;
• to reason why something happened;
• to describe what they are seeing, hearing, feeling and doing;
• to imagine or create fictional characters or events;
• to chat to other people and respond to their ideas;
• to ask questions;
• to give instructions.

Talking with others

Give children the opportunity to talk to different audiences:
• another child;
• adults;
• a small group of children;
• the whole class.

These situations require increasing confidence. Many children are happy to stand up in front of their class and sing a favourite rhyme or talk about a recent event. Others may be reluctant. Never force shy children to perform in front of a large group as it may put them off for life. As they watch others, they will gain the confidence and the impetus to talk in their own time.

Some of the opportunities mentioned arise naturally as children play with peers, but others need to be planned. Gathering in small groups where children share and discuss the work they have done can be fruitful. Encourage the children to listen to each other, to offer ideas and to extend their language skills.

Language in context

Stories and story-telling

Story-telling is an oral skill with its roots in the personal anecdotes, jokes and incidents that are part of daily conversation. Stories may entertain or inform but their power lies in their ability to enthrall the listener. When telling stories to young children, make sure that the ending is positive. It does not necessarily have to be the usual 'happy every after' ending, but it should leave them feeling secure and confident.

Story-telling develops children's listening skills. It also allows children to visualise or imagine scenes, characters and events. Story-telling also gives children an idea about story conventions, for example, the development of characters, situations and plots.

Traditional and familiar stories

However well-known a tale may be, each story-telling produces a new story. You are not restricted by the author's words; you can create your own version. You can adapt the characters and sequence of events according to your intentions and the interests of the children.

Young children particularly enjoy stories that refer to familiar events that they have experienced. For example, the story of 'The Little Red Hen', which gives scope for a detailed description of bread-making, can be told after the children have made and tasted a loaf of bread. When we did this in my nursery, the children contributed plenty of words and ideas, and the reference to the smell of warm bread baking in the oven made their mouths water.

You can also change the story to emphasise aspects that you feel are important, to reflect your own personality and how you see events. Folk tales are particularly suitable for telling as they are part of our oral tradition. Before the tales were written down, each teller reshaped the story to reflect the people and events of the time. There are, therefore, many variations of traditional tales. For example, in some versions of 'The Three Little Pigs', the pigs are eaten by the wolf; in others, they are saved by the third pig. Both versions are equally valid. It depends on what feels right for you and your audience.

Developing children's listening skills

Story-telling is interactive. You and the children face each other. The children are drawn to your face and respond to direct eye contact. You can use your own facial expression and intonation to portray characters and atmosphere. This helps children to understand unfamiliar language and to visualise characters and events. Often without being aware of it, you adapt the language, scene and events of the story to the children's interests.

Persuade the children to show their listening skills by:
• participating in refrains, such as 'Run, run as fast as you can, you can't catch me, I'm the gingerbread man';
• participating in lists of characters or events such as, 'The little old man, the little old woman, the cow, the horse...'.

How to make the most of a story

• Choose a story that you enjoy. It is easier to start with a well-known tale.
• Sequence the main events, for example, in 'The Gingerbread Boy', the sequence is (a) making the gingerbread boy, (b) the chase, (c) meeting the fox and (d) the outcome.
• List the main characters as they appear: the man, the woman, the gingerbread boy, the cow, the horse and the fox.
• List any repeated phrases.

• Imagine the characters and scene. In a few words describe a scene, for example, the smell of biscuits baking, or an event, for example, the gingerbread boy jumping out of the oven.
• Include direct speech, for example, 'The little old woman said, "I will make a boy from gingerbread."'
• Practise. Look in a mirror to make sure you are making the most of facial expression and gesture. The younger the children, the more they respond to exaggerated gesture and intonation.
• Keep events, characters and description to a minimum.

Choose a familiar story and give it a try. It is well worth the effort. Try adapting traditional tales, for example, your tale could feature a gingerbread girl who outwits the fox.

Story props

Use items such as toys, a head-dress or puppets to illustrate the story. These help children to visualise and remember characters. An old blanket over your shoulders will evoke an old woman, for example, Red Riding Hood's grandma. However, do not let the props define the character too closely. They should act as a springboard for children to use their imagination and should not confine it by representing the character in too much detail.

The following items can make effective props:
• clothes from the dressing-up box, for example, hats and shawls;
• objects that are featured in the story, for example, a turnip or a frying pan;
• puppets made from paper bags or wooden spoons;
• finger puppets made from felt, fabric or card.

Story-boards

A story-board provides a different way of presenting a story and acts as a support to the story-teller.

To make a story-board, cover a board with felt or similar fabric. Cut out simple characters from pieces of felt of different colours. These will cling to the covered board. Alternatively, paint an old metal tray or biscuit tin lid so that the characters will stand out. Cut out characters from card. Stick a small commercially available magnet on the underside of each figure so that they cling to the metal tray.

As you tell the story, place and move the characters on the board.

Involving children in stories

It is important that children feel that stories are not just events that happen to other people in other places. They need to see them as part of their own daily lives. This will help them to create stories using their own experience of places and people. In this way, rather than just repeating other people's stories, they will realise that they can make their own. Encourage this by making up stories in which the characters and places are familiar to the children.
• Take a familiar toy, for example, a doll, and make up a series of stories featuring adventures that happen during the course of play.
• Tell stories based on a shared event, for example, a local visit.
• Invite children to be the central characters of the story.

• Invite children to tell stories about events that have occurred at school or at home.

Choose your own adventure

Encourage children to participate in making up stories. This will make them realise their own capacity for story-making. Take up children's ideas and develop the story accordingly. There are various ways of encouraging participation.

• Ask the children to name and describe characters.

• Let them offer alternatives for the next action, for example, does the gingerbread boy run across a field or down the street?

• Ask 'What could happen next?' At first, children will make suggestions based on former stories but they will soon appreciate their role in decision-making and start to control the outcome of the story.

Children's own stories

In the early years, children are introduced to a wealth of cultural experience. Give them the opportunity not only to listen to the stories of others but also to make up their own.

We make up stories every time we sort, select and arrange our actual and imaginative experiences. Provide children with the resources to make up stories in all areas of the nursery. These stories are the sequences of action that occur during imaginative play with sand, water and construction equipment, as well as in the role-play area. Encourage children to describe the events taking place as they play so that they become aware of their ability to create stories.

Early stories may be elusive and lacking in coherence, but listen carefully and watch the children's actions to help you understand the story framework. You can write down the action stories and read them to others.

Make available a wide range of resources for imaginative play, including some of the following:

• Water and sand. Include small figures, animals and vehicles to encourage children to make up stories. Observe as children use small twigs, cones and feathers to represent figures.

• Small construction toys. Include small figures, animals and vehicles. A building shell with no defined function will be used by children as a garage, hospital, house or boat. Such a building encourages them to use their own imagination to the full.

• Scrap materials. Provide cards, wrapping paper and catalogues with figures to cut out. Let the children use their own imagination to create vehicles and figures to use in imaginative play.

• Clay and dough. Listen to the stories children tell as they shape and mould these materials.

Role-play

Role-play stimulates children to become actively involved in make-believe. The child pretends to be someone else and somewhere else in a fictional situation. The whole of the child becomes wrapped up in this new character, moving and talking in a new way. Role-play does not rely on acting techniques but rather on the ability to look at a situation from another person's point of view.

At first, the child imitates and reproduces activities that she has seen in others, for example, pouring tea. Later, she draws on her own experience and imagination to create characters, situations and action. The child must really believe in the character to play the role to the full. As

role-play is firmly rooted in children's experience of situations and people, it is important to extend such experience. Invite people, possibly parents, to talk about their work and to demonstrate the equipment or skills they use to the children.

In her early years, a child responds and thinks only as an individual, but over a period of time she learns to participate and think as a member of a group. Dramatic play provides the motivation for children to co-operate with others. As children share the same situation and objects in a familiar yet fabricated context, for example, a pretend shop, they learn to share their play. Two children playing alongside each other with a tea-set may offer to pour tea for each other. Children learn to make decisions, give and follow instructions, and use language to reason, report, predict and project.

Attitudes and relationships that can be found in the home will be reflected in the child's play. The parts she acts out may have strong emotional undercurrents that allow her to express unspoken and unconscious feelings. Drama gives form and expression to both experience and emotions. Observe and intervene sensitively to support the child as she

recreates and comes to terms with her feelings. Any behaviour that may cause particular concern should be reported to the appropriate agency.

Your part in role-play

You need to observe children's role-play and take your lead from them. By picking up statements and signals from the children, you can assume a role, perhaps that of a customer, and help to develop their play. In your role you can show them that dramatic play is valuable and worthwhile. You can also provide a model for children to build on. The 'customer' may be friendly, ill or in need of help. This will challenge children's attitudes and encourage them to dig deeper into their experience for a response.

Using toys

Those children who find it difficult to relate and interact with their peers may find it easier to use a toy as the focus of their role-play. Dolls are often cast as babies, but other toys can be used effectively. Large child-size teddies can play the parts of patient, sister and friend. They are passive and do not make demands on the child. Use a child's keenness to bring toys to life to

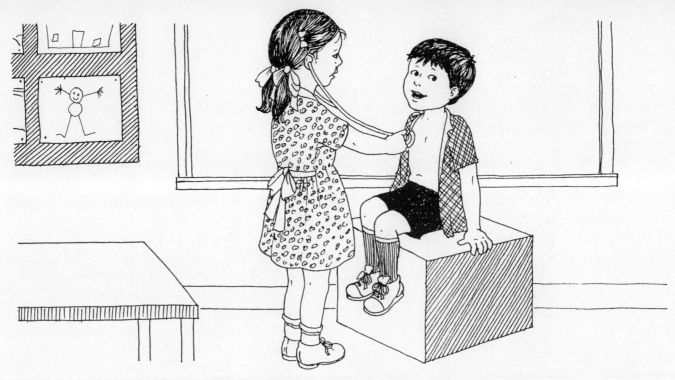

encourage role-play before she is ready to negotiate and co-operate with others.

The role-play area

The role-play area should stimulate children to create their own imaginary situations and characters. Effective role-play provision:
• offers scope for children to initiate characters and situations;
• offers unlimited scope for interpretation, that is, it may be a boat, a house or a plane, according to the children's intention;
• offers scope for children to arrange and select their own requirements;
• attracts both boys and girls.

The home corner is the traditional focus of role-play. It usually centres on the kitchen area, and this determines both the nature and structure of children's play and your expectations about how they will use that area. Kitchen equipment has specific functions and it produces a predictable and often repetitive sequence of activities that make few demands on the child's imagination. The kitchen area is often associated with female activity and is often chosen by girls.

To counter this, it is important to choose items with undefined uses that can represent an indefinite number of objects. For example, large, open cubes could

become a cupboard, a cooker or a window, or they could be used to build a wall. A few real objects will help to add the finishing touches. Make resource boxes available with equipment for 'shops', 'homes' and 'hospitals'. Let the children select the necessary equipment. Shapeless garments such as overalls that are easily adaptable to many situations are more useful than identifiable clothing such as police uniforms. Keep an eye on gender implications in the choice and use of equipment. Select the equipment carefully and review and change it when necessary.

Resources for the role-play area

Equipment should reflect our multicultural society, and should not perpetuate gender stereotypes.
• Try to provide enough space for children to organise and arrange their own equipment. You may have to limit the number of children playing in this area at one time to avoid over-crowding and encourage co-operation.
• A carpet helps to absorb sound.
• Invest in a screen to divide one 'room' into two.
• Large open cubes or blocks that are size-related will allow children to build their own environment.
• Provide materials which encourage

literacy, including books and writing materials.
• Provide some large heavy-duty boxes full of resources for different environments, for example, a shop, a hospital and a house. Stick picture labels of the contents to the sides to enable children to sort and return equipment.

Here are some ideas for filling the resource boxes.
• *'Shop' box:* a till, used ticket rolls, a wire basket, a shopping basket, a purse, plastic or real money and home-made cheque books. Add brochures from large stores, hand-outs, posters and notepads to make lists.
• *'Baby' box:* new-born sized baby dolls representing different races, a selection of real baby clothes and equipment that parents no longer require, for example, sleep suits, feeding equipment and blankets. Make sure that you include clothes for boys and girls. Add a clinic card and books to read to the baby.
• *'Kitchen' box:* a set of size-related pans and lids, plates, mugs and cutlery. Include food utensils from other cultures, for example, a wok. Supply recipe books and

set up a pretend cooker top. A wipe-off memo board is also useful.
• *'Vehicle' box:* small traffic cones, road signs, a lollipop sign, luminous jackets, maps, road-user books, pads and pencils, a steering wheel, tubing for use as fire pumps, a medical kit, a diary and an appointment book.
• *'Dressing up' box:* an assortment of fabrics, possibly old curtains, that are cut into different large shapes, for example, squares, triangles, rectangles and circles to use for clothes, blankets or picnic table cloths.

Also include a variety of hats, jackets, overalls and other garments which can be used for different roles.

Rhymes

Skipping and action rhymes are part of children's oral learning and they can often be heard in the playground. Children delight in their compelling rhythm and rhymes. Using rhymes in the classroom is a good way of drawing children's attention to the sounds of words. They allow children to stand back from commonly-used words and listen to their sound out of context. Jingles and rhymes allow them to play with words, an important part of their language development.

When children have a firm grasp of the way the world works, they particularly enjoy nonsense rhymes which present a topsy-turvey world, such as 'Higglety, pigglety, pop! The dog has eaten the mop.' (Traditional rhyme, collected in *Tiny Tim*, illustrated by Helen Oxenbury, selected by Jill Bennett and published by Armada Picture Lions.) Words are treated like objects that may be explored and played with. This ability to stand back from words is a crucial factor in developing reading and writing skills. Children need to be able to transfer the continuous sounds of speech into separate units or words in order to write them on paper. Identifying the spaces between the words and the sounds that make up words is the key to further literacy development. Playing with words by saying

rhymes helps children to stand back from speech. Traditional rhymes are the way that our culture passes these skills to its young children, as these rhymes emphasise sound rather than sense.

Invite children to sing the words to songs they know, and introduce new ones. There are four basic types of rhyme commonly used in the early years classroom.

Nursery rhymes

Most nursery rhymes are very old and were not originally written for children. They have their source in ballads, riddles and customs. They are rooted in the rural life of past centuries and feature people who will be quite unfamiliar to many modern, urban children, such as pipers, shepherds and tailors. Many of the rhymes are archaic and make little sense, but they are still popular.

Circle rhymes

These rhymes, such as 'Here we go round the mulberry bush' and 'Farmer in the den', invite children to co-operate as part of a

group. You can adapt the words to extend their use. For example, using the tune of 'The Mulberry Bush', you could describe nursery activities, 'Tim made castles in the sand today'. Let the children contribute their own verses.

Action rhymes

Action rhymes such as 'The Scarecrow' (in *Oranges and Lemons* by Karen King, Oxford University Press) require children to respond using their whole body.

Finger rhymes

With finger rhymes such as 'Tommy Thumb' and 'Here is a basket' (both in *Round and Round the Garden* by Sarah Williams, Oxford University Press), the children have to respond with their arms and hands to represent the objects.

Poetry

Rhymes and jingles are particularly suitable for young children, but you can also read them poems that evoke an atmosphere or event to which they can relate. Children enjoy listening to cadences within poems such as 'Duck's Ditty' by Kenneth Graham (in *The Book of 1000 Poems*, Unwin Hyman) and 'The Train Goes Running Along the Line' by Clive Sansom (in *Tiny Tim* by Jill Bennett and Helen Oxenbury, Armada Picture Lions), even though they may not understand some of the ideas. Tape record poems and rhymes that children enjoy for them to use in the listening centre.

Television

Television provides a source of stories, songs and information for young children. Many children watch a good deal of television and you should use it sparingly in the early years classroom. However, a relevant programme can be a useful educational resource.

Discuss programmes with the children after you have watched them together. In this way, watching a television programme becomes an active rather than a passive occupation.

Radio and cassettes

The radio and pre-recorded cassettes provide stories, rhymes and music for listening to. Often, children find it difficult to listen to a disembodied voice; they rely on a visible context for much of their understanding of language. However, they will be more willing to listen to stories and songs they know in a listening centre. Place the accompanying book by the cassette player so that children can associate the story with the book. This will encourage them to match the spoken words with the pictures and print. They will probably enjoy even more listening to tapes of your voice with its familiar tones. Make tapes for the listening centre of a group of children singing rhymes and songs.

A story cassette

Make a cassette recording of a story for the children to play in the listening centre. Begin by greeting the children and introducing the story, giving its title. Then tell the story, putting as much emphasis into your voice as you can. For example, try to use a different voice for each character, and add some simple sound-effects. At the end of the story, remind the children to switch off the tape.

At the end of the tape, you might also like to offer the children some ideas for their next activity. For example, you could suggest that they make a model or paint a picture based on the story.

Computer work

There should always be at least two people working on the computer, either you and a child or two children. This will ensure that ideas are discussed and language is developed. The best programs to use with young children are those that encourage problem-solving and present the children with challenges, such as hiding and finding an object.

Your role

Your role in stimulating language development can be summarised as follows.
• To accept and value the accent and mother tongue of each child.
• To encourage talk across the curriculum.
• To create situations and provide equipment that encourage talk in an imaginative context.
• To provide conversation partners, both adults and peers.
• To encourage talk for different purposes, for example, to recall, to predict and to imagine.
• To encourage children to listen to others.
• To introduce a variety of language structures including story, rhyme, non-fiction and poetry.
• To introduce and discuss media including television, radio and cassettes.

Reading

In families where parents read and write for work or leisure, children are constantly exposed to the idea of reading, whether for pleasure or through necessity. These children often ask for or are given the means to imitate their parents' activity, for example, they could have old order books to write on or be introduced to a word processor. Sometimes they will be asked for suggestions to write down, for example, 'What would you like to put on Clare's birthday card?' Parents will also explain what they are doing when they are reading or writing for a purpose. In these homes, literacy is an essential part of family life and children are expected to participate and become literate.

The early years classroom must carry on the work started in homes where participation in language and literacy is an essential and regular part of daily life.

What is reading?

'Reading is much more than the decoding of black marks upon a page: it is a quest for meaning and one which requires the reader to be an active participant.' (*English for Ages 5 to 16* [The Cox Report], HMSO 1989.)

The meaning of words should be the focus of reading activities with young children. We need to encourage them to understand written text. To achieve this, they must actively think about what they are reading. Encourage them to bring their own experience and expectations to the reading process.

The Bullock Report states that, 'there is no one method, medium, approach or device, or philosophy that holds the key to the process of learning to read.' (*A Language for Life*, HMSO 1975.) From the beginning, you must encourage children to use a variety of reading strategies, including prediction based on meaning and recognising words by sight, a useful skill.

Meaning and motivation

The most meaningful texts for children are those which they choose to read or have read to them. This may be a birthday card, a favourite story or the logo on a T-shirt. By asking for these things to be read, children are demonstrating an awareness of print, that is, recognising its form and realising that it communicates messages. This is a very important step.

Children are motivated to read in an environment which displays print and where adults use print for a purpose. They will model their behaviour on that of adults. Observe as they write signs, attributing their own meanings according to how they want to use them. They may write their own letter shapes to accomplish their goal, perhaps to name the boat they have made. James placed a string of magnetic letters on a board in front of his boat, saying, 'That says "Sharks! Don't eat us!"' As children become aware that written forms have a specific shape and follow rules, they may ask you to write notices for them or to read existing ones.

Print in the early years classroom

The forms of print

In the school or nursery you need to display many different types of print.
• Display a range of logos and signs. Many examples of packaging and shop signs will be familiar to children. The names of popular toys are usually easy to identify so

that children recognise and read them in catalogues, on packets or on television.
• Consider media advertisements, which present lettering that moves, expanding and shrinking, or changing into a picture or pattern. This sort of print is colourful and often irregular, with an almost infinite variety of shape and size. For many children, this is their first contact with print. Reflect this print in the classroom by writing bold, colourful and attractive captions.
• You will probably have many examples of the black regular print of books, forms and newspapers. This is the most common type of print in school, whether it is in books or on computer print-outs.
• Let the children see various examples of handwriting, which has individual characteristics of style. For example, you and other staff can write lists and captions for the children, or you can provide old envelopes with addresses for the children to use when they are pretending to be postmen.
• The words which appear on the screen of a word processor are an increasingly important part of modern communications. Children need to be introduced to word processing as early as possible.
• Display a variety of different types of print in the appropriate places. For example, put up a sign in the toilet area to remind children to wash their hands. Reading in the nursery should reflect the forms of reading in the community. Children can begin to recognise print in all its forms and use their knowledge of reading at home and at school. Just as children eventually recognise a dog as a dog, whatever its breed, colour and size, so eventually the children learn to recognise and identify letter shapes, whether they are printed, handwritten or designed using sophisticated graphics.

The functions of print

Show the children how useful print can be. Make them realise that reading is an enjoyable leisure activity by bringing your own books into the nursery to read. You will probably read very little of them, but they could stimulate discussion about

reading and books. Show your enthusiasm and interest in children's books by your willingness to read stories. The enjoyment found in a book sustains a child when reading seems to be an uphill struggle.

We can also obtain a great deal of useful information by reading, and it is important for children to realise this. Read recipe books when baking with the children. Follow written directions for games and read the instructions for using equipment. Children who understand that reading is useful and serves many purposes are motivated to read.

The book corner

The book corner should attract children to books and reading. Make sure that it offers a variety of colourful picture books. Choose shelves that display books at child height and face out, so that children can see the covers.

Make the corner comfortable so that children can relax and enjoy books, and be willing to read stories, especially when you are asked. Provide a selection of toys, puppets and story-boards to encourage children to tell favourite stories and make up their own.

Carpeting, cushions and seats encourage children to sit or lie and look at books alone or with friends. Posters at child height, featuring story characters and favourite rhymes written using rebus, that is, substituting pictures for words at key places, will also encourage reading behaviour.

Print everywhere!

Children need to see print, not only on the walls and in the book corner, but throughout the classroom. Consider each area and provide appropriate reading material.
• In the construction area you could leave a range of maps, tourist brochures and books about vehicles, buildings and bridges.
• In the food area, supply recipe books, information books and leaflets about foods such as fruit, flour and milk.
• In the role-play area, provide appropriate reading material for each environment. For example, supply some junk mail, newspapers and circulars for the 'home' box, and travel brochures for a travel agency.
• If you have an 'office' area, leave out some telephone books, catalogues and order forms.
• On the investigation table place appropriate fiction and information books on the topic under investigation, and write labels and captions beside the items on display.

Print in the environment

Print of different colours, types and sizes features prominently in the streets, on hoardings, in shops and on television. Children soon learn to identify the logos and packaging of favourite items and places, such as sweets and hamburger restaurants. Associating print with a particular object is the first step towards reading for many children. Give the children this first type of reading material so that they can continue to interpret and talk about familiar signs and print. For many children, it will bridge the gap between reading at home and reading at school. Children need to see that print has a meaningful and useful role not just in school but at home, so that they do not get the idea that reading is just something they have to do at school.

Present packing and other print to the children in a variety of ways.

• Make scrap books of print from food packaging. Invite children to make individual books of their favourite foods by bringing in packaging of their choice. Class or group books can be based on general topics such as 'breakfast time', where cereal packets and bread wrappers are supplemented with pictures from glossy magazines. Write down the children's comments alongside the packets. These books are popular and provide valuable talking points as children identify packages and relate them to their everyday lives.

• Feature everyday packets on investigation tables as points of interest. For example, a hamster- or rabbit-food packet, empty if necessary for safety reasons, can stand alongside the nursery pet.

• The scrap materials box is a valuable source of everyday packaging. Many children are attracted to familiar packets and will enjoy looking at the print and pictures as they design and make models.

• Include relevant environmental print throughout the nursery, such as calendars, desk diaries and posters in the office. Junk mail, catalogues and telephone books can be included in the home corner.

• In the role-play area, include signs and labels that are part of everyday life, such as posters indicating sale items in the shop, or examples of hairstyles with a price list for the hairdressing salon. Many shops are willing to give away old display notices. You can also make signs and labels, perhaps to indicate a bus stop or the name of a space ship.

• Captions on the wall can reflect the colours, sizes and shapes of environmental print. Use thick felt-tipped pens to make the print colourful and attractive.

• When visiting shops or any other area, draw children's attention to prominent notices, signs and labels. Read them with the children and discuss their importance.

• Make shopping lists for the food area, using labels from food packets so that children can identify and match them. When you are out shopping, discuss the contents of other packets as indicated by their labels. It is easy for children to distinguish flavours of yoghurt, jelly and whipped desserts, as many packets feature the fruit.

All kinds of books

Reading stories

'Whatever else the pupil takes away from his experience of literature in school he should have learned to see it as a source of pleasure, as something that will continue to be a part of his life.' (*A Language for Life* [The Bullock Report], HMSO 1975.)

Stories are a strong motivating force. When a child enjoys a story, she is drawn to the book it came from to recreate the satisfying story experience for herself. In doing this, she turns her attention towards

71

print and reading. The enjoyment of stories creates an interest in books, which stimulates a child to read. A prime objective for early literacy, therefore, is getting children to enjoy stories.

Stories demand children's physical, emotional and intellectual commitment; they need to sit still, empathise with the characters and create the story world in their imagination. The words and pictures act as a springboard for their imagination. Stories help children to create possible worlds and to become aware of the use of symbols. This idea is the basis of future learning.

Stories bring the close and undivided attention of an adult, which gives children a sense of security and emotional well-being. Sharing stories promotes reading for pleasure and encourages children to learn to read for themselves. It also provides an invaluable opportunity for parents to be involved in their child's reading.

Reading for information

Encourage children to look for information in non-fiction books. There are many simple but clear information books that you can read to children. Some of these deal with events in a child's life, such as going into hospital or having an eye test; others are concerned with the outside world, such as the production of milk or the life-cycle of a hen. Many have colour photographs to support the text.

The style and tone of most non-fiction books differ from story books. Facts are presented in a clear, concise and logical sequence. Some non-fiction books, however, use the style of a story to present facts in a more enjoyable way. For example, a book outlining the production of milk may feature a character visiting a farm, the factory and then delivering milk to the supermarket or home.

Suggest non-fiction books as a source of information at appropriate times so that children will appreciate how useful they are. For instance, the children may be studying caterpillars in the minibeast tank and may need more information on them. Questions that children raise can be answered by turning to non-fiction. Make it clear to the children how to use the books, for example, by saying, 'Let's read this book to find out what we want to know about caterpillars.'

Picture books

Picture books are not just books with illustrations; they present a story through pictures and print working together. The pictures convey atmosphere, character and setting, and can sometimes indicate a sub-plot. Facial expressions reveal feelings, as in *Titch* by Pat Hutchins (Picture Puffin). Sometimes the pictures tell one story while the words tell another, as in *Rosie's Walk* by Pat Hutchins (Picture Puffin). In this book the words relate the hen's view of her walk around the yard before tea. The pictures show the fox that tries unsuccessfully to catch the unwitting hen.

Pictures can also extend a text. In *Maisie Middleton* by Nita Sowter (Picture Lions), the pictures introduce a new character, Maisie's teddy. This teddy amuses the reader by imitating Maisie's actions. In

You'll Soon Grow Into Them, Titch by Pat Hutchins (Picture Puffin), the background illustrations depict growth in nature, and we watch flowers bloom and birds hatch as the story unfolds.

Wordless picture books encourage children to tell the story in their own words. This is quite challenging. At first, children pick out details that are relevant to them and just name them. Later, the children will follow the central character through a sequence of related actions. In most books of this type, the pictures follow a left-to-right sequence and this helps the children to develop a sense of the direction of print. Wordless picture books are a useful way to introduce the idea of a story and books to children as they rely on you to interpret the scene according to the interests of the child.

Some picture books use 'oral' language, that is, they reflect the patterns and structures of everyday speech. These books are often about everyday events such as washing or shopping. Sarah Garland's books *Doing the Washing* and *Going Shopping* (Picture Puffin) feature a colloquial phrase on each double spread to help children relate to the story. There are some interesting child's-eye views, for example, from the rear seat of the car.

Other picture books encourage children to participate actively, for example, *Where's Spot?* by Eric Hill (Picture Puffin). This book uses oral language in the direct questions addressed to the reader: 'Is he in the cupboard?' The child has to find the answer by lifting up flaps on the pages.

Patterned language, which features rhythm and rhyme, is popular with children who respond to the sound of words. These memorable and predictable rhythms and rhymes support the child when he retells the story. *Each Peach Pear Plum* by Janet and Allan Ahlberg (Picture Lions) is an example of this.

Comics

Find a place for comics in the book corner. They are part of popular culture and many children are familiar with them. Many comics feature television characters whom children recognise quickly and to whom they relate. Some of these characters, for example, Postman Pat, also appear on television and in books. Some story writers use the comic-strip technique in conventional picture books. The 'Meg and Mog' series by Helen Nicoll and Jan Pienkowski (Picture Puffin) features comic-style bubbles for speech and colourful print. This style attracts children to reading and books.

Encouraging reading behaviour

Favourite stories

A story's most valuable attribute is the pleasure it brings to young children, who often ask for a favourite story to be repeated several times. Children follow the pages of a book as you read. Each reading confirms the child's expectations and yet teaches them something new about books and reading. Children become familiar with the arrangement of a book, the format of a story and book language. They also become aware of the types and arrangements of print. Moreover, they actively look for meaning in the pictures and print.

Children who turn to books for pleasure will be motivated to read. Each reading of a favourite story brings the child closer to the text and print. As he becomes familiar with the words and the pictures, he starts to retell the story in his own words, page by page. He is beginning to behave like a reader, which is an important step in learning to read.

Picture cues

Encourage young children to use picture cues when telling stories from books. The pictures are a vital source of information. For young children interpreting the

pictures is their first form of reading. Pictures and print are both symbols; that is, they represent something else, although print is the more sophisticated symbolic system. Children have an idea of what reading is all about when they look for the meaning in pictures and photographs. Discuss pictures and help children to sequence stories to develop their idea of story structure and book language. You will need to name new items which are represented in the pictures, and introduce new language structures.

Interpreting pictures

Picture books should be visually attractive, and for young children they should have bold illustrations, strong colours and little or no background, to make them easy to interpret.

At first a child relates a person or object to its photograph or picture. He does this with family photo albums as the child recognises himself, his family and toys. Producing a book of photographs of the nursery or classroom is always popular.

Young children like to identify and name people and objects that they recognise. At this stage, they enjoy looking at home and toy catalogues which feature familiar objects. *The Baby's Catalogue* by Janet and

Allan Ahlberg (Picture Puffin) encourages this interest.

Children need experience of interpreting pictures before they can assimilate what is relevant. A double page spread, with a picture of the same character on each page, can be confusing. 'That's the boy and that's his brother,' said one child, trying to make sense of the pictures. Pictures which show only part of a person or animal can also be confusing for young children.

As they gain more experience of books, children will enjoy spotting familiar or amusing features in a detailed picture. As children identify with pictures, it is important to take into account the implications of race and gender when you choose picture books.

Book conventions

As they become familiar with a story, children will want to 'read' the story to themselves or a friend. As they read you can observe how much they know about books and print. Encourage them to 'read' stories to you and to each other. A large soft toy in the book corner makes a cuddly and patient audience for the children.

Examine how well the child can use the book and relate to the print.

• Can she find the front of the book?
• Does she position the book correctly?
• Does she turn pages over one at a time?
• Does she proceed from front to back?
• Does she point to the words as she tells the story?
• Does her finger go from left to right? Later, you may see the return sweep of the finger. At first, children often proceed from left to right, and continue on the next line reading from right to left.
• Does she use the spaces between print, that is, does she allocate one spoken word to one written word, although the match may not be correct?
• Does she read the left hand page and then the right hand one?
• Does she read from the top of the page downwards?
• Does she start to recognise familiar letters or names and comment on them?

Book language

As children retell stories they reveal their understanding of book language. There are certain phrases associated only with stories, for example, 'Once upon a time'. This phrase announces the beginning of a story. When they are familiar with the phrases, children repeat them. Certain phrases provide a refrain, for example, 'He huffed and puffed and blew the house down.' Refrains give the story a pattern and help children to remember it.

The characters in a story are usually described in the third person, and the action in the past tense. Most children use the present tense when they talk, and speak about themselves or others using 'I' and 'you'. They need to understand that the pronouns in a story stand for imaginary characters and that events are described as having already happened. Children also need to appreciate that the terms denoting time and place, such as 'there', 'here' and 'then' refer to the story world. Once when I read a story containing the words, 'come here' to some young children, one child actually stood up and walked towards me.

It takes a while for children to assimilate the language of books. The more they hear stories, the more they start talking like a book. Listen as a child 'reads' stories.
• Does he include common story phrases such as, 'Once upon a time'?
• Does he repeat familiar phrases such as, 'He huffed and he puffed'?
• Does he use the third person where relevant?

• Does he use the past tense confidently? When children know that the past tense is needed, they will often invent words by applying endings they know to new words, for example, 'they goed to the woods'.
• Does he use familiar story conjunctions such as 'and then...'?
• Does he use terms of place and time in the story context, for example, 'here', 'there' and 'now'?

Children soon become word-perfect and will correct a hurried or careless reader.

Reading and rereading

When children ask for their favourite stories time after time, this gives you the opportunity to draw the child closer to the text. You can show them book handling skills, the direction of print and the way spoken and written words match. You can talk about stories generally and the conventions of print. This sort of language about language is often termed

'metalanguage'. It is a vital part of learning to read, as adults often refer to 'letters' or 'words' and expect children to understand. It may however confuse a child who is unaware of the new meaning of a familiar word. For most young children, a letter is something that arrives through the post.

Introduce language features as you read, but remember that the enjoyment of the story is the priority. Introduce only a few terms at a time where appropriate, following the child's interest and answering his questions. As you read the story, talk with the child about the conventions of reading.
• Name the parts of the book, for example, the cover, the pages, the top of the page, the bottom of the page, the next page, the pictures and the print. This helps to consolidate book handling skills, which include finding the start of the book, holding the book the right way up (orientation), and turning over one page at a time.
• Talk about print, for example, the difference between words and letters, the first letter and the last letter. The concept of a word or letter is very difficult for young children to understand. Spoken words flow into each other and young children find it hard to differentiate between words and parts of words. Show them the spaces between written words.
• Talk about story conventions, for example, the beginning of the story, the end of the story, where the story starts and the title.
• Introduce the idea that print reads from left to right by pointing at the words as you read. Children become accustomed to watching the left to right direction and will imitate it when they retell the story. At first, children imitate the direction with no reference to the words, but later, they start to take account of the fact that what they say should begin with the first word and end with the last. This shows that they are starting to match the written word with the spoken word. Later, they use the spaces between words and any initial letters or sight words they know as a guide.

make books based on favourite rhymes, for example, 'I'm a little teapot'. Encourage a child to expect a meaningful text, by asking 'Does that make sense?'

Use all the appropriate reading strategies. Encourage a child to look at the picture as a guide. It takes practice to interpret pictures. When children make predictions about what will happen next, reread previous words to give them the idea of the text. Then read the rest of the extract and discuss any past predictions.

Introduce the idea of sight words, perhaps the name of a character or a repeated action. Ask, 'Have we seen this word before?' The first word a child reads is often his name. Provide plenty of opportunities for children to practise this by writing their names on cloakroom pegs, name cards and milk tickets.

Introduce the idea of letter-sound correspondence using letters that children recognise, perhaps from their name.

Big books

Big books with enlarged text and pictures are suitable for sharing with a group of children. Many of these become favourite stories which can be used to introduce the idea of picture and context cues. They often have texts with patterned language, that is, rhyme, rhythm or repeated phrases, to help prediction.

Read the books and point to the words, inviting the children to participate. This will then encourage them to make predictions. Let the children read these big books in unison, each contributing as much as they can. Many children feel less threatened if they are part of a group and are more willing to take risks and try out their guesses. Children who are familiar with the story may offer to read the book to the group, demonstrating their knowledge of books and reading behaviour.

Making a big book

Make a large-format book by folding large sheets of thick card or heavy-duty paper in half, and sewing them together down the

Reading strategies

Reading is a very complex process, but we can encourage children to think when faced with a text. From the beginning, introduce children to context cues and to reading strategies. When introducing a new text, ask children to predict what might happen. In the middle of the story, ask them to guess what the next words will be. This will encourage them to draw on their own resources of language and meaning to make sense of the text. It also lays the foundation for reading strategies. Present it to them as an enjoyable challenge. Accept their guesses, saying, 'It could be that, but actually it says...'. Support the children's attempts to make sense of text. A child's motivation to think and make sense of print is more important than the correct answer.

Make use of context cues, including grammar or syntax. Encourage a child to use his knowledge of speech to predict the next words. Ask, 'What do we say next?', and, 'How do we say it?' To encourage this,

Eventually, the child takes over the main role, while the adult offers any necessary support. The child's role varies according to his familiarity with the book and his reading ability. Young children may memorise the story and later feel confident enough to 'read' it. Whatever happens, the enjoyment of the story is central.

There are several advantages to shared reading.

• Sharing a story with someone they love makes children feel emotionally secure and gives them something to look forward to. The same feelings are associated with shared reading. The child also has the full attention of an interested adult who will answer questions.

• Shared reading provides an opportunity to read and contribute at the child's own level without giving her any reason to worry about not saying the correct word.

• Regular periods of shared reading build the foundations for a lifetime's reading and give children an extensive experience of books.

Browsing

Give children the opportunity to look at books in a relaxed way. Books of all types, story, poetry, rhyme and non-fiction, should be available for children to choose and look through at their leisure. Books that are familiar invite children to recreate the story experience for themselves. Watch them as they tell a favourite story to themselves or a toy. This allows them to practise their book handling and reading skills. An enjoyment of books paves the way for regular silent reading. Ask adults, possibly volunteer parents, to read stories on request, to listen to children's retellings and to talk about books.

fold using a strong needle and thread. Cover the seam on both sides with carpet tape to make it more hard-wearing.

Choose a favourite rhyme or story, and write one phrase or sentence on each page. Write boldly so that the text is easily visible, and be creative in the way you present the text. For example, write words which indicate size, such as 'tiny' or 'huge', in appropriately sized lettering, and use felt-tipped pens in the appropriate colour when writing colour words such as 'red' and 'green'.

Shared reading

Shared reading takes place when an adult reads a story with the child. This can be done on a one-to-one basis at home or using big books with a group of children at school. The adult and the child read the text aloud together. Initially the adult provides the main voice, with the child contributing as and when he can. Later, when the child has more confidence, he is willing to take over more of the reading.

Talking about books

Talking about books helps children to become selective readers. Encourage children to discuss which books they like and why. Remind them of the different stories and ask them about the ones they

enjoyed. Talk about favourite characters that reappear in different stories and recall their adventures. Ask them to choose a story that you can read together.

At the end of a story, invite children's comments on the characters or plot. Ask open questions to encourage a personal response, such as, 'What did you like best?' Directed questions are useful once children start talking about the book, 'Oh yes, I remember. Now what was his name?'

Responses to stories

Let the children respond to a story in a variety of ways:
• verbally, discussing characters and events;
• in pictures, using pencil or paint to draw a favourite character;
• by modelling with clay or dough, or using scrap materials or construction equipment;
• in movement, recreating a favourite rhyme or story using their body;
• in writing – some children prefer to retell the story in writing either using their own letter shapes or by dictating the text to you.

Your role

Your role in guiding children towards good reading habits can be summarised as follows:

• to create an environment where books and reading are enjoyed and valued;
• to share books with children on a regular basis, encouraging children to participate and answering their questions;
• to give children a wide experience of many types of books and opportunities to browse and talk about books;
• to demonstrate reading to children and encourage them to take part;
• to encourage children to use a variety of cues and develop reading strategies, so that they use whatever is useful and see reading as a problem-solving activity;
• to give children the space and time to read alone, encouraging silent reading;
• to involve parents in developing their child's reading skills.

Ideas for parental involvement

A home library

Although most children may have books at home, not all parents can afford a well-stocked library that caters for their child's growing thirst for books. A visit to the public library may involve an expensive or difficult bus journey, particularly for parents with more than one young child. At one time, only children who could read

were allowed to take books home, so that the very children who needed books most were denied them. Having seen the enthusiasm with which parents and children choose books, particularly those with restricted resources, and the benefits to children in terms of familiarity with stories and a positive attitude towards books, I am convinced that home libraries are an essential feature of the nursery.

Setting up a library

You will need to provide a low shelf or book box to display the books. You will also need a wide range of quality children's books, including fiction, poetry, rhyme and information books.

Library cards

Any library needs an efficient system for recording which books have been borrowed. In my nursery, which offers part-time places, children who come in the morning have a card of a different colour from those who come in the afternoon. This makes for easy referencing. Morning cards are kept in one box and afternoon ones in another, and there is a pencil attached to each box.

Each card has the child's name and picture label so that the child can find his own card. There are three sections on each card, one for the date, another for the title and the last one for parents' comments about the book and about their children's progress.

Borrowing books

Parents and children are invited to choose a book together. This encourages them to browse and talk about books. The child usually looks for his borrowing card in the box and the parent writes down the title and date.

Returning books

Parents write down their comments on the card as they discuss the book with the child. A new book is then chosen and added to the list. The books can be changed at any time.

I advise parents to keep favourite books for a longer period so that they can be read several times, and to return those that are not liked as soon as possible.

Protecting the books

The library books have pieces of bright sticky tape on the spine so that they can be distinguished from the children's own books. The children are given a plastic sleeve with their name on to protect the books.

Shared reading

To make the most of the home library, it is worthwhile informing parents about reading in the nursery as soon as their child first starts. It is also useful to produce a brochure that parents can refer to later. Keep the brochure simple and clear; parents can always ask you for further information.

Writing

A writing environment

A child's early writing is often termed mark-making. It is important that children develop the skills of composing, gathering and sorting their ideas at the same time as they develop the skill of writing them down.

Create a positive writing environment in the nursery by:
• providing the materials and the encouragement necessary for the children to make marks;
• having an interested adult willing to write down children's words and messages;
• creating situations where writing is purposeful and useful;
• having an adult to provide a model of writing behaviour.

Children need to be aware of the different functions of speaking and writing. We speak to another person or group of people who respond with nods or words that indicate that they have understood. When we talk, we use our hands, voice tone and facial expression to help carry the message. Most people find it easy to speak. Writing is more difficult to produce. We need to think carefully before we start, to ensure our message will be understood, as the reader is rarely present to give any feedback. A written message needs to be carefully composed to ensure that it requires no further explanation. However, a written message may be read by any number of people and even sent long distance. When we speak, our message disappears as the sound of the voice fades. By contrast, a written message can be referred to at any time.

Introduce children to the idea that all the words we speak can be written down. Write down the children's own spoken words and read them back. To demonstrate this further, you can also write down and read messages from the children to others, captions for paintings and drawings, labels for display, conversations in role-play, and the children's own stories and songs.

The writing centre

Set up a writing centre with materials to help the children explore the functions and forms of print.

- Provide a variety of mark-making equipment, including pencils, crayons, chalk, charcoal and felt-tipped pens. Offer different types of paper in many colours and sizes to make writing attractive, and include a range of different fasteners, such as a hole punch and wool, a small stapler and rolls of sticky tape.
- Leave out a range of everyday materials to encourage writing, such as diaries and order forms. A supply of used envelopes, used stamps and stamps cut from sticky paper will encourage children to write letters. Provide a post-box made from a cardboard box, too.
- Create a context for literacy with an office environment, including telephones, desk tidies, trays, a typewriter and a word processor. Have a table, chairs and open shelves with boxes to allow children easy access to equipment.
- Give children their own personal book in which they can choose to write or draw. They can help you make these simple books from paper. Encourage them to choose a way of fastening them.
- Provide cards showing names, letter headings and greetings for the children to use when they write.

The opportunity to write

Give the children an opportunity to write in all areas of the nursery, not just the writing centre. Let them try drawing and writing with fingers and brushes in paint and wet sand. Consider the potential for writing in each area. In the construction area, provide clipboards and files for making signs and placards. Alongside the scrap materials, place pencils, crayons and felt-tipped pens with which the children can draw figures, and write signs and labels for models. They can also use the pens to colour and write their own names on models. Tie a pencil on a string to each easel so that children can write their own names on their paintings.

A small stick or twig can be used for mark-making in the sand tray. Fingers are useful, too! Show the children how to make letter shapes with strips of dough when they are modelling.

In the role-play area, include writing materials appropriate to the setting, for example, put memo pads and catalogue order forms in the home corner.

The uses of writing

Create situations where you and the children need to write for a purpose.
- Writing to remember: write down the items you need for baking on a shopping list. Take this to the shop with the children and read it as you select the items.
- Writing to communicate: encourage the children to write messages for each other and for their parents. Fasten these to the noticeboard in the writing centre.
- Writing to communicate long-distance: write letters to other schools and send cards to children in hospital.
- Writing to record: write down children's descriptions and stories so they can be read another day.
- Writing to express ideas and feelings: encourage children to compose their own messages and 'read' them to you.
- Writing to sort ideas: introduce selecting and sequencing words in word processing (see pages 86 to 88).

Types of writing

Introduce children to the many different types of writing by writing with them. In this way, children's writing becomes their reading material. Invite groups or individual children to contribute to different types of writing, including the following:

• lists, for example, names of 'patients' in the 'hospital' or toys invited to the 'party';
• stories that children create in imaginative play, new versions of favourite stories and retellings of events in the nursery;
• traditional rhymes or made-up ones;
• descriptions of objects and living things, such as snails or twigs, many of which may have a poetic quality in the personal vision that they reflect;
• instructions which are useful in the role-play area: for example, 'Please wait here. You can read a comic', was a sign 'the hairdresser' had written for the customers.

In all these activities, children gain experience of the different types of writing and also a develop a sense of the audience to whom the writing is addressed.

Writing activities can be initiated by you or the child. For example, children may wish to make cards for relatives and friends. They may concentrate for a long time, absorbed in planning and accomplishing their tasks. They know what they want to achieve, but may need some help. Be available to offer any support and assistance they may need. One child may need help folding the card, while another, not yet confident enough to write his own message, may ask if he can dictate it to you.

Look for opportunities to initiate literacy activities. After a visitor has talked with the children, you could suggest that they write a thank-you card. Involve the children in planning the activity and they will soon take over. Invite everyone to sign their 'name' so that they all feel involved.

A sense of ownership

It is important that children can relate to the aims and forms of the print that they see around them, otherwise they may feel

that writing is for adults. Let them know that their own early writing, whatever form it takes, is valued. They are often only too well aware that their own 'writing' does not correspond with an adult's script. This can lead to a sense of failure: 'I can't write!' Children who feel they are unable to write do not bother to try. Practice makes perfect. Each time a child draws or writes, he is building up skills and understanding that take him forward to the next stage. Give children the confidence to continue.

Display children's early writing on the walls. Ask them to write labels and captions for their artwork. Encourage them to write their own names on paintings and models. Many children have a recognisable 'signature', and it is interesting to observe how it develops. Provide a noticeboard for children to display items of their choice, including things they have written.

A sense of audience

Writing for others and knowing that your work will be read is very important. By doing this, children will realise that writing is communication and not just an end in itself. This is an important concept, as it also demonstrates that writing uses standardised signs so that others can make sense of it. Children learn to appreciate the public nature of print and the need to learn letter shapes.

Before children can do this, however, you can act as scribe and write down children's messages. Many children will 'read' their own approximations, but you will notice that the message often varies with each reading.

Give the children a choice of audiences for their writing:
• parents and relatives;
• staff and helpers;
• friends;
• small groups and class groups;
• other classes;
• visitors.

Early writing behaviour

Making marks

Being involved in a literacy environment helps each child to construct her own theories about writing. She will have her own way of interpreting and expressing written forms. However, it is possible to follow the progress from early mark-making to conventional writing.

Discovery

A toddler, given a crayon and paper, notices the marks she has made. At first, these marks may be short and random (see Figure 1).

Figure 1

Control

Attracted by the colour and lines made by the crayons, the child concentrates for longer periods, guiding the path of the crayon and establishing control (Figure 2).

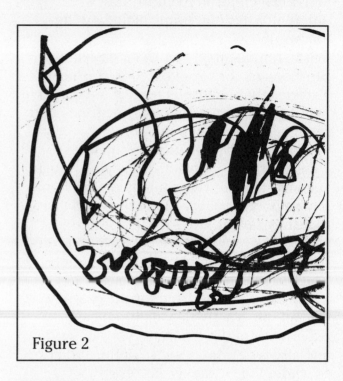

Figure 2

Experiments

The child will begin to experiment by making different marks. Some are repeated and some are changed. The marks will include spots, swirls, crosses and stripes (Figure 3).

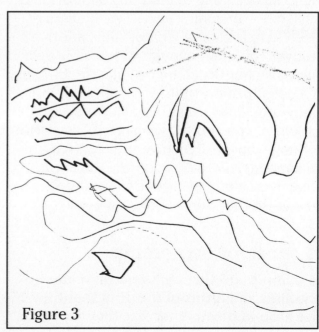

Figure 3

Signs

At any stage, a child may declare that the marks he has made are 'writing' or 'daddy', that is, they stand for something else (Figure 4). For many children, this happens when they draw a man who resembles a spider. This indicates that they can represent objects through drawing and are ready to tackle other symbolic systems, namely, writing. The circles and lines used to draw the man can be easily converted into letter-type shapes.

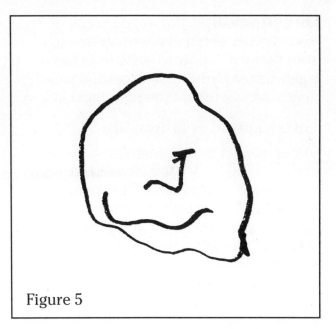
Figure 5

Figure 4

Letter-type shapes

Drawing and writing are closely associated when children start to make these shapes (Figure 5). Many children write an approximation of their name and say, 'I drawed my name'. They may draw a picture of themselves and write their name beside it saying, 'That's Katrina and that's Katrina, too.' Some may incorporate letters within their drawing, for example, in figure 5, Julian drew J for his name, drew a face around it and used the J for the nose. Other drawings can be peppered with isolated and random letter shapes. At this stage, children enjoy drawing letter shapes in paint and wet sand.

Letter strings

Children may then start to write rows of letter-type shapes (Figure 6). These may be horizontal or vertical. They will often repeat letters from their name several times, turn them round or change them in some way to make a new letter shape. They are often based on capital letters, which are easier to form. Children often like to watch staff write, looking on in fascination as the writing crosses the page. Watching staff also serves to reinforce the left-to-right direction of writing.

Figure 6

Directionality

You need to watch children writing to be sure that they know to write from left to right. Letter strings that cross the page may have started on the right-hand side.

Letter/sound relationship

Children start to relate letters with sounds and use these to write messages. These messages are a string of letter sounds, for example, 'BRD' was written on a child's drawing of a bird. One, two or three letters stand for a word which can be read by an informed reader.

Invented spelling

Children gradually start to represent all the sounds in a word or phrase (Figure 7). Several words may run into each other, for example, one child wrote 'HRZEPRZNT' for 'here is a present'. He was not yet aware of word boundaries and spacing. At this stage, children are interested in conventional spelling and often use sight words in their writing.

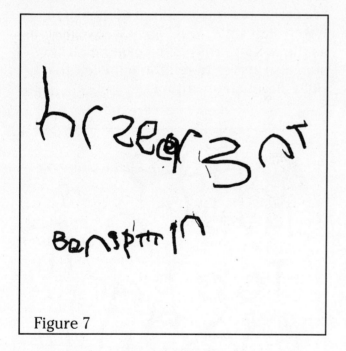

Figure 7

Conventional spelling

This is the eventual goal, and to achieve it children need to use their visual memory and their knowledge of letter/sound relationships and spelling rules.

Word processing

Word processing has many advantages. It helps to develop children's story-telling abilities, with the adult acting as scribe and keying in the story as the child dictates it. This also gives an opportunity to introduce oral drafting, as the child considers the words he has 'written' and decides whether or not they express what he meant.

It is important that children get an opportunity to watch others use the keyboard, and to use it themselves. You can use the word processor to produce many different sorts of text, from stories to posters, and this will give children experience of the various functions of print.

Shared writing

A standard infant word processing chip with large screen type, jumbo print and 'WYSIWYG' (what you see is what you get) facility is useful for shared writing. You may like to try some of the following ideas:
• Ask the children to say rhymes or tell stories for you to type (Figure 8). For example, Angela offered, 'Baa, baa black sheep, have you any wolf?' Repeat aloud what you are typing to emphasise the association between speech and typing.

Twinkle twinkle little star
How I wonder what you are
Up above the sky so bright
like a diamond in the sky

nicholas

Figure 8

• Read back both the words on the screen and the printed version. Do not assume that children will make the connection between the two.
• Give the children a copy of their work. They may like to illustrate it or make their own letter-like marks on it.

We saw a little
dog outside
the shop.

• Publish the material in books, on noticeboards or walls. Display print wherever handwriting is traditionally used. However, do not let it completely replace handwriting on display. Word processing should not diminish the importance of children's own mark-making, but it does offer further opportunities for you to act as a scribe.

Oral drafting

When you first introduce children to word processing, type and print what they say without changing any of it. Any intervention may break their concentration and prove counter-productive. Children soon learn that whatever can be said can also be typed. Let them take their printed copies to other adults for them to 'say it' and confirm what they have dictated.

As their experience increases, encourage children to develop their ideas. Ask questions such as, 'Tell me more about what happened when you went shopping', and, 'What else did you do at the seaside?', to prolong the story. At other times, ask them to describe a character more closely, 'What did the dog look like?' Develop a

promising story-line with, 'What happened next?' Do not try to replace the child's own text, but encourage her to enhance and extend it.

Discuss where and how the new extracts can be included, and read the passage through again to show the child how it sounds now. Children will understand that by using a word processor they can change and improve their first version.

Using the keyboard

Under your supervision, let the children explore the keyboard.

At first, let them press keys and print out the result. Children enjoy simply pressing the keys and watching the letters appear or disappear as they use the delete key. Some children may attach meaning to these letter strings, calling one 'a letter for mummy' and adding, 'What does it say?'

Type the child's name on each piece of work. It is useful if name cards have a printed and written version of a child's name. Just as children imitate the letter shapes in their name when mark-making, so they try to identify the keys on the word processor that are used in their name. At this stage, children appreciate the need to press the key correctly to type only one letter. This requires great care and attention but most have the will to succeed.

Most children will contribute the first letter of their name. This soon becomes a letter string. As a child starts to use visual discrimination instead of just memory to locate and identify a letter, she may press incorrect but similar keys, for example, an L instead of a J.

When a child can type her own name, she starts to type those of her family and friends. Introduce the space bar at this point, as it now becomes useful and relevant. Realising that upper case letters on the keyboard produce lower case ones on the screen does not usually cause problems.

Let the children watch as you use the keyboard. After she had watched her teachers, Emma used the keyboard to tell a story. She told the story slowly, pressing a key with each syllable. She even made 'mistakes' and deleted and replaced single letters, imitating her teachers. Her story resembled the letter strings of early mark-making. While Emma typed, I wrote down her story by hand.

The concept keyboard

The concept keyboard has the potential to develop whole-word recognition. Make overlays using pictures from catalogues, shapes cut from felt or real three-dimensional objects. When children press the picture on the keyboard, the appropriate word appears on the screen.

You can also use the keyboard to encourage discussion. For example, provide a picture of a rabbit and the word 'likes', followed by a choice of pictures, including a cake, an apple and a banana.

Alternatively, use children's photographs, possibly from the sample roll left by the school photographer. On pressing the photograph, the child's name will appear on the screen.

Your role

Your role in helping a child write can be summarised as follows:
• to make the forms and purposes of writing explicit;
• to encourage the child to participate in writing activities;
• to act as scribe so that the child's own ideas can be written down and read by others;
• to encourage children to explore and experiment with mark-making;
• to provide situations where writing is useful and relevant;
• to introduce the word processor and the idea of drafting.

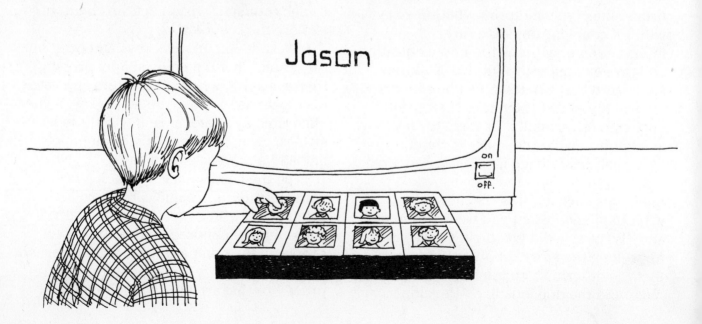

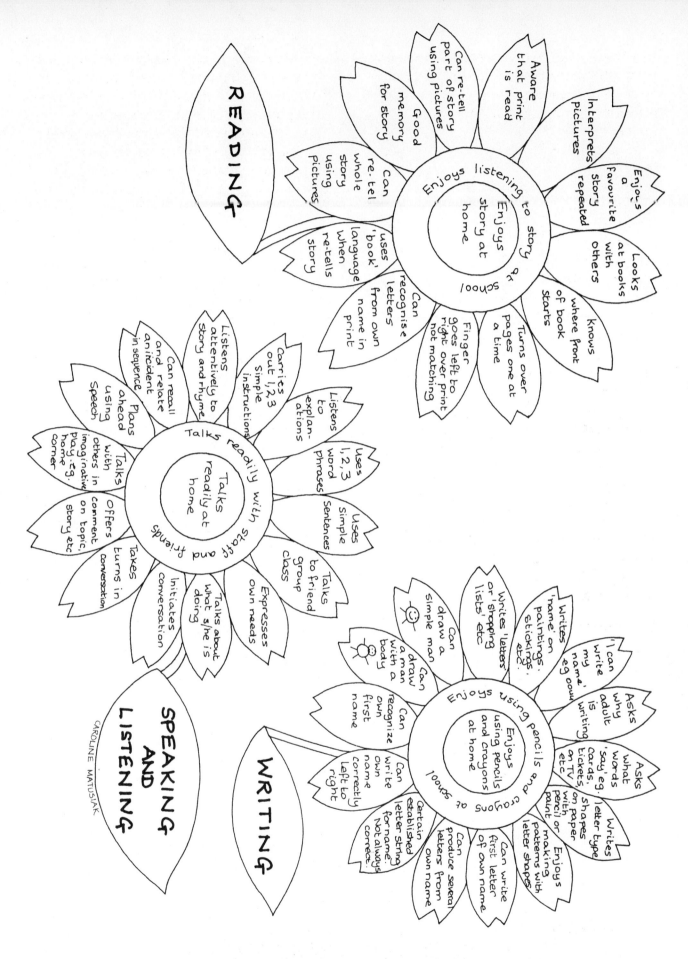

READING

Enjoys listening to story at school
Enjoys story at home

- Aware that print is read
- Can re-tell part of story using pictures
- Interprets story pictures
- Good memory for story
- Enjoys a favourite story repeated
- Can re-tell whole story using pictures
- Looks at books with others
- Uses 'book' language when re-tells story
- Knows where front of book starts
- Can recognise letters from own name in print
- Turns over pages one at a time
- Finger goes left to right over print not matching

SPEAKING AND LISTENING

Talks readily with staff and friends
Talks readily at home

- Listens attentively to story and rhyme
- Can recall and relate an incident in sequence
- Carries out 1,2,3 Simple instructions
- Plans ahead using speech
- Listens to explan-ations
- Talks with others in imaginative play. e.g. home corner
- Uses 1,2,3 word sentences
- Offers comment on topic, story etc
- Uses Simple phrases to friend Group class
- Takes turns in conversation
- Expresses own needs
- Initiates conversation
- Talks about what s/he is doing

WRITING

Enjoys using pencils and crayons at school
Enjoys using pencils and crayons at home

- Can draw a simple man
- Writes 'letters' or shopping lists etc
- Can draw a man with a body
- Writes 'name' on paintings, stickings etc
- Can recognize own first name
- 'I can write my name' eg oouu
- Can write own name correctly Left to right
- Asks what words say. eg. on TV, on paper etc
- Asks why adult is writing, tickets, Cards, shapes letter type
- Certain established letter string 'for name'. Not always correct.
- Can produce several letters from own name
- Can write first letter of own name
- Enjoys mark making with pencil or paint
- Enjoys pencil or letter patterns with letter shapes

CAROLINE MATUSIAK

This page may be photocopied for use in the classroom and should not be declared in any return in respect of any photocopying licence.

89

Chapter 4
Mathematics

'Direct experience, for example of handling materials and making constructions, inevitably increases children's understanding of ideas about order, difference and quantity. Their ability to use mathematical language discriminatingly and accurately is increased through well planned practical activities and play experiences....' (Her Majesty's Inspectorate, *The Education of Children Under Five*, HMSO 1989.)

Maths in the early years is largely based on practical activities and experiences. With careful planning, it can become an integral part of the nursery's routine. Everyday chores associated with organisation, including preparation, tidying up and registration, can be shared with children. This encourages sorting, shape and number. Most activities involve an element of maths; for example, painting entails covering an area. You can develop this further by providing paper and three-dimensional boxes of different shapes for painting.

Maths is about relationships of number, size and shape. Children need to explore these in a meaningful way so that they develop a fascination for maths. In applying maths to achieve a personal or shared goal, children develop useful strategies such as logical thinking, problem-solving and estimating. These, in turn, require accuracy. For example, an estimation for a headband that proves too small leads to looking at ways of measuring.

Attitudes to maths

Children who regard maths as a useful tool will develop a positive attitude towards it. By planning activities, you will encourage children to use maths creatively and systematically. As children share

experiences they will use maths as a form of communication to describe, predict and interpret. Their concentration and persistence will be rewarded by the satisfaction of achievement.

Maths and parents

Give parents the information they need to participate in the mathematical development of their children. Often, parents who appear unwilling to become involved, simply lack confidence. When questioned, parents may state, 'Oh, it's all different now. I don't want to confuse her,' or express a dislike for the subject. Parents who understand and enjoy maths pass on their pleasure to their children.

Inform parents about how maths is taught in the nursery; for example, how children sort materials as they tidy and how shapes are used and explored as children build with bricks and scrap materials. Let parents know how they can help in the nursery. Assisting with the

computer and baking are useful ways of getting parents involved in activities which have a considerable mathematical aspect.

Tell parents how they can help their child at home. Display brochures or posters listing ideas for sorting, matching and counting with everyday items. For example, children might help with sorting and matching pairs of socks.

Ideas for parental involvement

Games and jigsaws

Parents can help their child's mathematical development by playing games with them at home. This encourages children to take turns and follow simple rules as well as using their knowledge of number and shape.

Jigsaws require children to match, order and fit shapes together as well as encouraging their visual discrimination. Young children find it easier to tackle tray jigsaws, as the border sometimes gives them a picture clue to help them start the puzzle.

Other ideas

• Start a games and jigsaw library. Parents are often willing to donate unwanted games and jigsaws for school use.
• Start a 'swap-shop' where children can exchange games and jigsaws.

Giving children confidence

Young children need to develop a positive attitude to maths to ensure that they approach the subject keenly and not with a sense of anxiety that inhibits learning. Children who enjoy maths and develop a sense of achievement from it show that they are interested in it. Those who see the relevance and purpose of maths in everyday activities are motivated to learn more.

Create situations where maths is necessary and easily applicable. It may be a

shopping trip where you use money to buy goods for the nursery, or it may be an imaginary shop in the role-play area. Let children participate in and observe these maths activities and give them the opportunity to imitate adults' use of mathematics and discover how maths is used.

Gender and maths

There is some concern that girls show less interest in maths than boys. Although we do our best to involve both sexes in caring and constructing, in reality many girls choose family role-play activities while boys choose construction equipment. Imaginative family situations where girls are encouraged to build, measure and count could help to persuade more girls to use construction toys.

Here are some different ideas for home role-play:
• Encourage children to construct household machines using large boxes.
• Invite them to use scales for measuring their own weight, or that of a baby or some food.
• Work with them to construct a milk bottle holder with a clock to indicate the number of bottles required, and provide some plastic bottles to count and place in the holder.

LEGO and other construction materials are traditionally associated with building vehicles such as cars, planes and boats. Girls may show more interest in building a pram to fit the LEGO baby or a trolley to push hospital patients.

Forget any preconceived ideas you may have about activities that boys and girls choose. Instead, introduce new contexts for play that will develop all the children's interests. In some cases, children's interests mirror the toys and games they have at home, which are often a reflection of parental expectations. Discuss with parents the importance of letting their daughters play with construction equipment as well as dolls.

Applying maths

Young children's understanding of maths will develop as they become more involved with the world around them. Be aware of the mathematical potential of everyday activities and base the children's learning on them.

The activities that children participate in teach them not only about mathematical concepts, but also how maths relates to everyday life. Children will learn to understand the importance of number as they count the eggs, of time as they wait for a cake to cook and even of fractions as you divide an apple into equal parts. Children who experience maths as a meaningful and integral part of everyday life are more likely to develop positive attitudes.

Mathematical activities can be applied to a variety of situations, for example, when children are building models, when decorating the role-play area, in games such as 'snap' and dominoes that involve shape and number and in trails looking for shape, number and pattern.

Problem-solving

'The ability to solve problems is at the heart of mathematics' (*Mathematics Counts* [The Cockcroft Report] para 249, HMSO 1982).

Real and imaginative contexts provide situations that demand solutions. For example, children may be making a building to house a certain number of dolls or teddies. Give children the time and encouragement to tackle problems for themselves.

Solving problems often involves investigating alternatives to discover the most effective solution. As they look at alternatives, children use maths creatively. They use mathematical processes to solve the problem: defining, estimating, predicting and testing.

Strategies

Real tasks encourage children to think mathematically, and a specific goal motivates them to go through several processes.
• They will try different materials and select the most suitable. Children involved in making bridges will place bricks of different lengths over two pillars until they find the one that fits.
• They will estimate. Children who have explored with LEGO and other layer systems can cover a base board accurately, with no pieces overhanging the edge.
• They will look for pattern. Children need a wide range of activities and materials in which to look for regular behaviour or other patterns.
• They will reason. Exploring materials gives children the opportunity to arrive at certain conclusions. It is important that you encourage them to arrive at their own conclusions. One child stated that a brick did not fit 'because it is yellow' but another brick did 'because it is red'. When I looked at the bricks, I noted that the yellow bricks were one size and the red bricks another. This shows that we need to listen carefully to children's conclusions. It also demonstrates that we need to evaluate equipment to ensure that it does not confuse children.
• Children will make and test hypotheses. Young children use their conclusions in later work. For example, a child who believes that red bricks are shorter may choose a red shape from a different set of equipment only to find the opposite is true. Give children a variety of materials and experiences to try out and modify their assumptions.

Logical thinking

Young children are capable of logical thinking. Most parents recognise how astutely children select sweets based on their estimation of the greatest size, length or number! Their judgements are perceptual, based on the senses, and relative, compared with other objects or features. In the same way a child can identify a sphere by feeling and seeing the curved surface and comparing this with the flat corners of a cube.

Adults have some absolute codes which do not depend on perceptual inference ≈ in other words, which cannot be worked out by simply using the evidence of the senses. However, we all use some relative codes, for example, it is easier to remember the length of 5cm when we compare it to the length of a thumb.

Children distinguish properties of shape and size by relating the object to its setting. They are, therefore, learning from their perception of the world. This relationship between perception and understanding emphasises the need to give children a variety of sensory or first-hand experience. Handling and seeing objects in a variety of settings brings a distinct impression of shape or size that lays the foundation for future abstract ideas, for example, the idea

of a sphere. Rolling a ball on grass or down a slope, handling an orange and making a ball with dough or clay gives young children the opportunity to investigate the features of a sphere.

The language of maths

Maths is a form of communication. Its language is precise and we cannot assume that young children understand it. For example, to many children a 'take away' is more likely to mean a pizza than a sum. Introduce mathematical language in situations that are meaningful to children. This may be on an individual basis or in groups.

As individual children handle and look at objects, introduce relevant mathematical terms, for example, when working in the sand or water tray, refer to full and empty containers. As groups of children co-operate on joint projects, introduce relevant mathematical terms. For example, use the word 'tessellation' when building with large blocks.

Mathematical ideas associated with number, shape and measure can be found throughout the early years classroom. Children may refer to such concepts without actually understanding them, so it

95

is important to give meaning to the words they use as well as to introduce new concepts. Their questions also reflect how much they understand and where their interests lie.

Talking with peers helps children to describe what they are doing and refine their concepts. Discussing shared activities encourages children to express their ideas, and this provides a form of recording. For example, Malcolm checked the sign in the construction area to see how many children could play there. 'Four!' he said, and started counting the children, touching each one, 'One, two, three, four! You can't come here, Lisa.' 'But I'm four. I had a birthday,' replied Lisa adamantly. 'But only one, two, three, four here,' declared Malcolm. 'Not *birthday* four.'

A maths environment

Children learn mathematics from situations which are practical, meaningful and purposeful, and in which the associated mathematical terms are introduced. It also helps if groups of children are working and talking together.

The situations you provide may be real, such as a shopping expedition for a baking session, or imaginary. Imaginary situations have the same potential for learning as real ones, since they also present a coherent framework. Devise interesting situations or contexts where maths is relevant and where children will be keen to learn.

Make the classroom a place where maths is used and applied in all areas. In the role-play area, create opportunities to use maths in an imaginative way. For example, imaginary shopping activities can introduce ideas of money and weight. Do some baking in the food area. This introduces the idea of time ('When will the bread be ready?') and fractions ('How many children want a slice?').

In the modelling area, moulding a piece of dough gives experience of shape and space. Printing with three-dimensional objects such as blocks introduces the idea that shapes have faces which may themselves vary in shape.

In the office area, let children use different sizes and shapes of paper. Outside they could explore height by climbing and distance by running.

96

Many stories introduce number in an imaginative context, for example, 'The Three Bears'.

Your role

• To devise meaningful real or imaginary contexts where maths is relevant.
• To introduce associated maths language to individuals or groups.
• To plan an environment where maths is useful in all areas.
• To encourage children to participate in everyday maths, for example, counting the milk or dinners.
• To encourage strategies such as estimating and looking for pattern.
• To encourage perceptual judgements and logical reasoning.

Number

Number names

A lively way to introduce number names is by singing counting rhymes such as, '1 2 3 4 5, Once I caught a fish alive'. Saying rhymes makes children familiar with number names. Use fingers or objects to represent the number as you sing the rhyme. You can count claps, steps and jumps, doing the action as you say the number name.

Introduce counting backwards by pretending to launch rockets, saying, '5 4 3 2 1 lift off!' Make a large rocket with a low step for each astronaut to stand on in turn. Count backwards together, and let the astronaut jump off into space.

Use rhymes such as 'Five currant buns', where a bun is removed each time. 'Five little ducks went swimming one day' is another popular rhyme which involves counting backwards. You could also read stories, such as *Ten, Nine, Eight* by Molly Bang (Julia MacRae/Puffin), where objects or people are removed.

Counting

The fact that children can recite number names does not imply that they can count. Counting requires a one-to-one match of number name to object. Watch as a child counts ten small toys. She may start by touching each object and saying a number name, but it is likely that one or more objects may be missed or counted twice before she finishes.

Give children plenty of opportunity to count with you. Touch each object as you count to establish the match between the number name and the object. Children need to learn that we count each object once. Some children become adept at one-to-one correspondence and continue matching beyond their knowledge of number names, so they have to make up number names as they go, such as 'nine, ten, twenteen'.

Numbers and sets

Invite children to make a set or form a collection of objects that are similar or that belong together. They should also be able to spot differences between objects, naming colour, shape or size.

At tidy-up time, ask children to sort equipment according to picture labels and return it to the appropriate boxes.

Treasure boxes of buttons, shells and small toys encourage children to sort objects according to their own criteria. These may not always be evident to an adult. The criterion may simply be to make a collection of objects they like.

Let the children sort a collection of soft toys or clothes into groups according to different criteria, possibly colour or size.

Ask them to sort scrap materials and put them into appropriate containers.

Matching one-to-one

Children need the opportunity to match one-to-one or, in other words, to compare sets. Matching helps children to recognise relationships such as 'more than', 'less than' and 'the same as'. Here are some suggestions to give the children:
• match people to plates in role-play;
• match one figure to each vehicle in the construction area;
• match one brush to each pot on the easel;
• match one button to each hole on a coat;
• match one shoe to each foot;
• match one cherry to each cake;
• match one coat to each peg.

Comparing number

Encourage children to estimate the number of objects in two groups, perhaps knives and forks in role-play, and to compare the number, that is, whether there are more or fewer knives than forks. Let them check this by setting the table and placing a knife and fork with each plate. This will help them to understand relationships such as 'greater than'.

There are plenty of opportunities for composing numbers of things. For example, the number of aprons near the water tray determines how many children can play there. Ask the children to estimate at a glance whether there are any spare places. Sometimes there will not be enough aprons; at others times there will be some left. In the same way, signs indicating how many children can play in each area give children the opportunity to count the people on the sign, read the number and

count each other. By doing this, they are comparing the number of figures on the sign with the number of children. There may be more children than figures, and they will need to count to ensure that there are not too many people there.

Threading beads and reels of different colours will also allow children to count and compare number.

Number activities

Odd and even

Children need the opportunity to make pairs, and to see what happens when this leaves them with an 'odd one'. Use natural pairs that children can relate to easily, for example, gloves, shoes and socks. Gloves drying on racks and piles of shoes and boots in the cloakroom will need to be paired before the end of the session, and this will give the activity a purpose.

You could also use sets of gloves, socks and bootees in different colours to fit the nursery baby. Ask the children to sort and match them on washing day. You could also introduce domino games where animals or objects have to be matched.

Conservation of number

Children need to realise the fact that if, for example, there are three toys on the table, it does not matter which order they are in, there are still only three toys. This concept is called conservation of number. To help with recognition of this concept, it is important that the numbers on dice or in games are not always represented by a regular pattern, but that the arrangement varies.

Give children lots of opportunity to count, particularly in small numbers, as they play. This helps them to build up a concept of 'three' and 'two'.

Ordinal numbers

On a relevant occasion, introduce the numbers that express order, such as first, second and third. This could be when you are discussing a row of passengers in a model, 'The first man is looking out of the window, and the second man is reading his paper'. Touch the objects as you refer to them.

Reading numbers

The first number a child recognises is often her age. This will be familiar from birthday cards and cakes. Some children write their name followed by their age; it is an important part of their identity. Encourage children to:
• make badges with sticky paper featuring their age;
• make cards for each other;
• make a cake in the shape of a number to celebrate the birthday of a child or pet.

Draw the children's attention to numbers in the environment, perhaps by going for number walks around or near the school. Look for numbers on doors, clocks, clothes, vehicles, signs and labels. Point out the numbers around the classroom, too. There are many activities to encourage identification of number symbols.
• Ask children to identify and press the number keys on the computer.

- Make biscuits using number shape cutters.
- Make sandwiches in the same way.
- Display a clear number track at child height.

Number recognition games are useful for children who can already recognise some numbers, but they can bring confusion and a sense of failure to those who cannot.

Counting fingers

A young child who understands maths when using objects may be confused when confronted with written arithmetic symbols. Counting fingers provides a natural link between practical maths and written numbers. Fingers represent the objects and yet are objects in their own right. The following ideas will encourage children to use their fingers for counting.
- Use fingers to represent objects when saying finger rhymes such as, 'Five little peas in a pea pod pressed'.
- Play games such as, 'How many?' Ask the children how many small figures, bricks or toys there are on a table and encourage them to use their fingers to represent the number.

Writing numbers

Children need to appreciate the relationship between written numbers and real objects. Encourage them to make their own written representation of a number of objects. Give them a pencil and paper and ask them to show on the paper how many objects there are. Make sure that there are fewer than five objects. Observe how the children represent the numbers and listen carefully to what they say. The ways of showing the numbers may include the following.
- An irregular pattern with no features that appear to relate to the objects.
- A picture. The child may draw the appearance of the object, perhaps its shape, colour or position, and repeat this for each object (see Figure 1). Some children actually draw round the objects at

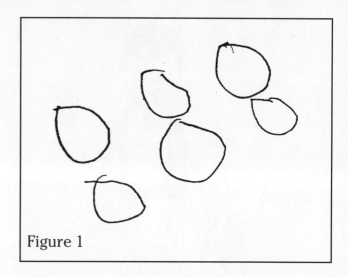

Figure 1

this stage. The children use their visual memory to draw the group of objects; they rarely say the number. When asked how many there are, they will count each drawing. Some children may be able to draw the correct number of objects, but are unable to count them accurately.

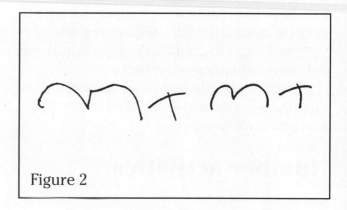

Figure 2

- A tally. In this case the child invents a mark to represent the object. One mark stands for one object (see Figure 2). These often take the form of tallies or single lines, possibly because they represent fingers. Some children hold up the number of fingers and then draw the lines. Other children may use letters (see Figure 2). Those who have a knowledge of number shapes will use those shapes and invent others as a tally. Some children write a number (1,2,3,4) to represent each object. This is still a tally as a mark is made for each object. These signs are abstract as they give information about the number and not the object.

100

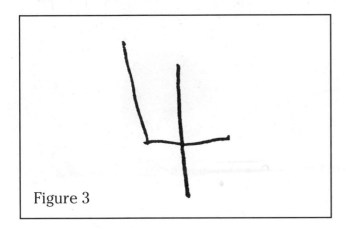

Figure 3

• Numbers. Eventually children use a single number to represent each group of objects (see Figure 3). This indicates that a child understands the relationship between quantities and written numbers.

Making a count

Give children the opportunity for writing numbers by providing equipment for writing in each area (see pages 81 to 82) and creating situations where number-writing is necessary. Children enjoy recording the number of pets or minibeasts in a tank, 'in case they run away and then we know how many we have to find'. Recording the number of children who want to taste a fruit salad will tell them how many portions are needed. In the role-play area, the number of patients waiting to see the 'doctor' can also be recorded.

Number operations

Children will be able to carry out simple additions and subtractions with numbers up to five, providing that they involve specific objects, people or events. Children are usually more successful at addition, and they achieve the total by counting on the required number.

Ideas for addition

• When one, two or three guests arrive in the role-play house, ask the children to add up how many cups there are and how many people. Ask them how many more cups

they need. How many people and cups are there altogether?
• In the construction area, use bricks, wheels and windows to add up.
• In the food area, count the number of people wanting to taste an apple or other food. This will introduce the idea of fractions as the whole apple or pie is divided into equal portions.

A number game

Stick a sheet of wrapping paper with a large picture on it on to a sheet of card, and cover it with clear sticky-backed plastic. Make a large die from a cube brick, and make number spots for each face from small circles of coloured paper. Put a range of small toy animals and play figures into a container – have about 20 little objects in all.

To play, ask the children to throw the die and count the number of spots on the uppermost face. Then they can take out the same number of objects from the container, and place them on the picture, either all grouped together or dotted about. After a few goes, ask the children to count the total number of figures. When different objects have been chosen, ask them to count the number of people and the

number of vehicles. Discuss the position of the objects on the picture, for example, by the tree, between the houses and in front of the flower.

Ideas for subtraction

• Five 'passengers' are sitting in a vehicle in the role-play area, but two leave. How many are left? Empty seats make this easier to visualise. Apply the same problem to many different objects and circumstances as the situation arises, for example, numbers of packets in the shop, baby clothing in the home area, and patients in the pretend hospital.
• In the food area, count the six eggs in a box, use two, and ask how many are left. Do the same with different foods.

Multiplication and division

By using objects in a meaningful context, children will be able to divide and multiply numbers.
• Ask them to share a quantity of currants so that each gingerbread man has an equal number of buttons.
• Soft toys, such as three bears, provide a good source of imaginative multiplication

and division. For example, 'Each bear has two socks, so how many socks are there?' and, 'Here are four sticks. The mother and father bear are going to carry them. How many will they each have?'

Your role

• To introduce number names by singing rhymes and sharing stories.
• To encourage counting on and counting back by singing rhymes such as 'Five currant buns' and playing games.
• To encourage children to record the number of objects, and to be aware of the systems they may devise to do this.
• To introduce the language for number operations as children play or as the situation demands.

Measures

Give children the opportunity to use measures in a variety of ways.
• Let them compare and order two or more objects, for example, two children standing back to back to compare their height.
• Ask them to measure with non-standard units, for example, encourage them to make

a height chart using handprints as units, and then stand each child in front of it and ask them to count how many prints high they are.

• Let them observe and participate in measuring accurately using conventional units, for example, when baking or making curtains for the role-play area.

• Give them a chance to explore standard measuring equipment, for example, rulers and balance scales, to get to know how they are used.

Concepts involved in measuring

Comparing

Measuring involves comparing two objects, either by placing them next to each other or by choosing a unit, perhaps a metre, by which to measure them both.

When comparing two objects, children need to look out for their differences and similarities. They need to be familiar with terms such as height, length, weight and depth. Introduce the terms for comparison too, for example, shorter than, taller than, heavier than, lighter than, wider than and narrower than. Children often use the words 'big' and 'little' to describe measure. Help them to define exactly what 'big' refers to by introducing the correct term, 'Yes, your wall is long'.

Ideas

• As children build with construction equipment, discuss their models introducing terms used in measurement, such as long, high, wide and so on.

• Outdoor play gives children the opportunity to experience slow, fast, high and low in terms of their own movements. Draw on this during structured play by asking children to move slowly or quickly, to jump high or creep low on the ground.

• During movement sessions, encourage children to stretch tall, stoop low and make fat shapes with their bodies.

Ordering

Seriation, or arranging objects in order of number or size, helps a child to understand the idea of 'more than' or 'less than'. Use three objects or people, for example, to introduce the idea of tall, taller and tallest.

Ideas

• Make silhouettes of equipment such as jugs and funnels in three graded sizes, and stick the silhouettes on the drawers or cupboards where the objects are stored, so that children match objects and pictures one-to-one and order them by size at tidy-up time.

• Read stories such as 'The three bears', which encourage counting and ordering by size. Make a felt story-board (see page 61) with figures and objects from the story and ask the children to match the bears to the appropriate bowl, chair and bed.

• If you provide three sizes of dolls in the home corner, this gives children the chance to match and order by size. Provide appropriate equipment, such as beds, covers and clothes so that these too can be matched.

• Invite the children to put three sizes of pans with fitted lids on their appropriate cooker hobs.

• Show the children how to put together inset puzzles with figures and shapes of different sizes.

• Provide stacking cubes and rings which have to be fitted together in a particular order.

• Provide three sizes of buckets for the sand tray to make pies.

Standard and non-standard measures

Introduce children to the idea of a unit of measure by using non-standard measures. Anything, from leaves to bricks, can be used as a non-standard measure. Start with a measure that is clearly defined and easily recognisable.

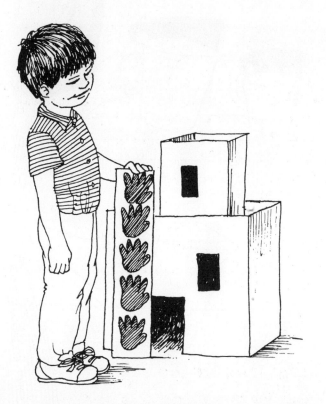

Non-standard measures provide a unit that children can see and handle. They make it easier for children to count and compare units. For example, make measuring lines with the children's footprints and handprints.

Children also need to watch how standard measures are used and then learn to use them themselves. Give them the chance to explore measures such as rulers, tape-measures and scales. By imitating how an adult uses these measures, children will show that they understand their function.

Introduce the names of standard units of measure, including gram, centimetre and metre, in a relevant context, for example, when making biscuits or dolls' clothes. Children will soon become familiar with the names of standard units and associate them with their application.

Length, height and width

Comparing

Place objects or people alongside each other for the children to compare their sizes. Introduce the terms associated with length, height and width.

Non-standard measures

• Use a row of objects to measure small items. For example, a row of LEGO bricks can be used to determine how many bricks long each object is.

• Make a height chart from prints made with bricks, hands or boots. Cut them out and mount them in a row from floor to ceiling to measure the height of children or large objects.

• Make non-standard rulers by sticking a few units, for example, handprints on to shorter lengths of stiff card. Cover them with sticky-backed plastic to make them more durable. Make measures of different lengths, for example, one, two and three units. Children can carry these around the classroom to measure smaller items.

• Introduce the children to measuring to fit. For example, measure the children for hats, belts and wristbands, using wool or string.

The children should place the wool round their waist or wrist, cut it to the appropriate length and use it to measure the card or fabric required.

Standard measures

• Show the children how to use a ruler, metre rule and tape measure as appropriate, when the opportunity arises during play.
• Introduce the metre rule. Place it alongside the height chart and discuss people and objects that are more than a metre and less than a metre high.

Depth

Comparing

Encourage the children to help you fill the water tray to different levels and discuss the changes in depth, using the words shallow and deep.

Non-standard measures

Ask the children to reach to the bottom of the water or dry sand tray and measure the depth, up to their wrists or elbows. They can also use a stick to measure the depth of water or sand in the tray.

Weight

Comparing

• Ask the children to compare the weight of an empty shopping basket with that of a full one, or an empty bucket with one full of sand.
• Let them feel and compare the weight of everyday items such as bags of flour, salt or sugar, packets of cereal, cans and kitchen rolls. You can do this during baking sessions.

Non-standard measures

• Use balance scales so that the children can watch how the pans rise and fall. Let the children feel and compare the weight of the pans.
• When asked to predict which is heavier – a packet of cereal or a bag of sugar – children usually think that the cereal is heavier as they make a visual judgement based on size. Let them compare a handful of shredded paper with a stone.
• Compare the weights of objects using a see-saw, so the children can observe how it falls with heavy weights.
• Use potatoes or stones as a unit of measure with balance scales. Items may weigh one, two or more potatoes or stones.
• Use pine cones, conkers or bricks as a unit of measure. Try weighing light items as well as heavy items so that children do not associate weight with size. What happens when you use feathers as a unit of measure?

Standard measures

• Introduce bathroom scales to the role-play area.
• On outings, let the children see how clinic or shop scales are used.

Area: tessellation

Measuring area involves measuring two dimensions at the same time, that is, length and width. Ask the children to cover an area with shapes that tessellate or fit together. Then ask them to count them. Start by introducing children to shapes that tessellate and those that do not.

Comparing

• Let the children print with different objects, perhaps including bricks, cotton reels and hands, to discover shapes that tessellate and those that do not.
• Encourage them to explore mosaics and tiles on baseboards to see which ones fit together.
• Using a set of size-related wooden blocks gives children an opportunity to discover which shapes fit together to make floors.
• Using different shape cutters with pastry or dough allows children to discover shapes that tessellate.

Non-standard measures

• Most children enjoy covering a LEGO baseboard with bricks. At first, bricks will overhang the edges of the board, but later children will choose and position bricks so that they cover the board accurately.
• Invite children to build models and stick on an assortment of small coloured paper shapes that may be cut or torn.
• Encourage children to place newspaper over the tables they will use for sticking and painting. This useful activity encourages them to cover an area with large sheets without leaving any gaps.

Standard measures

• Show children how to make curtains, bed blankets and other items that need to cover an area, measuring the areas required with standard measures.
• Encourage children to help put up displays which involve covering an area of board. You can measure the board together beforehand.

Volume and capacity

Volume is the amount of space an object takes up. An object's capacity is the amount it can contain. Objects with thin sides such as a beaker or a milk carton

• Let the children fill different containers using a measure such as a lid or a shampoo bottle.

• Ask them to fill a large item with a small measure and a small item with a large measure. What happens?

Standard measures

• Introduce some commonly used standard measures, such as spoonfuls and cupfuls. You could do this in a baking session where teaspoons and tablespoons are customary measures. Use recipes that measure in cupfuls and spoonfuls. Convert favourite recipes if necessary.

• Introduce the litre and half-litre when baking.

• Provide plastic litre and half-litre bottles, jugs, cylinders and trays for the children to compare. The litre measures should have the same shape as the half-litre ones, but a different size and capacity.

Time

The measurement of time needs to be introduced carefully. Children's first understanding of measuring time is probably linked with home and school routines, for example, tidy-up time and breakfast time.

Daily routines

It is useful if the nursery session has a general, but not too regimented, routine to enable children to recognise the passage of time. Name each part of the session, for example, home time or group time, so that children can refer to them. A familiar routine helps new entrants to settle. It gives them confidence to know that there is group time, tidy-up time and then Daddy arrives. Take photographs of the class at different times and mount them on cards for children to discuss and sequence.

• Many storybooks, such as *Sunshine* by Jan Ormerod (Picture Puffin), depict the daily sequence of events such as getting up, dressing and having breakfast. They are a useful starting point for talking about times of the day.

have a similar volume and capacity. Others, such as a plastic vacuum flask from a child's lunch box, have a different volume and capacity.

Children can learn about volume and capacity by filling and emptying containers in the water or dry sand tray. They can also learn about displacement, which is used to measure the volume of an object, by placing it under water and watching the water level rise. This method is often used with irregular shaped objects. Make sure that there are appropriate resources in the sand and water to explore this subject.

Comparing

Encourage the children to compare a range of containers, discussing their contents using terms such as 'full', 'empty', 'half full' and 'full to the brim'.

Non-standard measures

• Introduce the idea of measuring with containers such as jugs, lids and yoghurt pots, and let the children experiment to see how much water or sand they hold.

• Meal times are special for young children. Put cereal packets and other food packaging in the role-play area so that 'breakfast', 'lunch' and 'tea' can be served.

Clocks

• Put up analogue and digital clocks and refer to them during the day. They can also be used by the children as part of their role-play. If you refer to clocks and watches occasionally, you will introduce children to their function and terminology.
• Place a clock with movable hands in the role-play area for children to use as they reconstruct daily routines.
• Include old wrist watches in the dressing-up box for children to wear. They can look at the watches and use times they know or make up similar ones, 'It's ten five o'clock. Go to work.'

Days of the week

• Children can become familiar with the names of the days by repeating rhymes such as 'Solomon Grundy'.
• Certain days in the nursery may be associated with different activities, for example, music and movement on Tuesday. Refer to the day and the activity, 'Today is Wednesday and we are going shopping.'

Photographs of the activities can provide a basis for talking about days of the week.

Past and future

Children find it difficult to appreciate the passage of time. Introduce the concepts of past and future in a meaningful context.
• Phrases such as 'in a minute' and 'it won't be long' are probably a child's first introduction to the idea of future action. Baking introduces the concept of the passage of time. Putting cakes in the oven and waiting 20 or more minutes until they are cooked gives you plenty of opportunity to refer to time past and future.
• Growing seeds takes a longer time and concepts such as yesterday and the day before will arise naturally in conversation.
• Planning for an outing or party can also introduce the concept of future time. Children may refer to the proximity of their own birthday, 'Only three sleeps and it's my birthday'.
• Recalling an outing or party will refer back to past time. Photographs help children to remember and sequence events.
• Discuss families and the concepts of new, young and old. Invite babies and grandparents to meet the children.

Money

Money is a form of measurement in daily use.
• Shop with groups of children for baking ingredients. Let them exchange money for goods. They will hear phrases such as, 'How much is it?' and 'Here's your change.'
• Provide money and cheque books for the role-play area. Include equipment such as empty packets, a till and a shopping basket to encourage children to 'shop'.
• Give children the opportunity to handle real money when there is money to be counted or as part of role-play. They can sort and match coins into piles or rows and start to learn the names of coins.

Your role

• To give children the opportunity to compare objects for size, weight, etc.
• To introduce the function of measures by involving children in situations that demand their use, for example, baking, shopping and model-making.
• To provide imaginative and role-play contexts where the use of measures is relevant and appropriate.
• To provide and organise equipment to encourage children to seriate or order objects.

Pattern

Pattern underlies mathematical relationships and occurs in number and in shape. Encourage children to look for pattern in man-made structures and shapes, and in nature. Let them create their own patterns using a variety of objects and materials. Ask them to copy patterns that they or others have made, and to continue patterns.

Children should be aware that pattern is regular and predictable. Point out to them horizontal, vertical and diagonal lines and arrangements of shapes. Look for pattern in a variety of different environments.
• In the nursery, look at curtains, flooring, carpets and ceilings.

sheets to use as a background for display. Fabric crayons can be used to draw patterns on plain cloth, such as sheeting. Use this material for curtains, cushions and cot covers.

Exploring and sharing

Encourage children to make patterns as they explore the possibilities of shape and space. Let them make neck and wrist bands, belts and crowns by threading cotton reels, cut-up painted rolls and straws on to pieces of wool or string. This will give a purpose to their creation and continuity of pattern. Ask them to try threading bottle tops and shells to make musical instruments.

Ask them to work as a group on a collage or background for display. As they do so, they will need to copy and continue the patterns started by others.

Creating patterns

Provide materials for pattern-making throughout the nursery. Children can make patterns:
• with paint using brushes or printing with different objects;
• with bricks and construction equipment;
• with fingers, shells, pine cones and other objects in sand;
• with currants on biscuits and slices of tomato on flans;
• with fingers, rope, the ends of rolling pins and pieces of open-weave fabric (such as netting) in dough;
• with bottle tops, lids, coloured papers and other scrap materials.

Copying and continuing patterns

Create a pattern with the children for them to copy and continue. You could use beads, mosaics, small plastic shapes or other little objects. However, you should let the children see the potential for pattern in a wide variety of materials. Start with simple patterns, using items with different colours and shapes.

• Outside, consider fencing, roof tiles, brickwork and pathways.
• Look at the children's clothes for stripes, checks and spots.
• Look closely at the arrangement of seeds in fruit. Can the children find other patterns in foodstuffs?

Pattern for a purpose

Pattern can serve a practical or an aesthetic function. Encourage children to create and copy patterns for a purpose.

Certain patterns of brick bonding create strong walls. With large or small bricks, encourage children to build walls, enclosures and towers that are strong enough to use for imaginative play.

Most patterns are attractive to look at. Let the children print patterns on the underside of wallpaper (NB: make sure that it has not been treated with fungicide) and use this to decorate the role-play area. They could also print patterns on large

Computer programs are available which encourage children to copy and continue patterns. Many of these involve matching for shape and colour.

Your role

• To encourage children to look for patterns in the environment.
• To create situations where pattern serves a purpose.
• To give children the opportunity to create patterns in different areas of the nursery.
• To create patterns with children for them to copy or continue.

Shape and space

Everything has a shape. Children need to recognise the shapes of familiar objects, such as cars, furniture and toys, as well as natural objects such as leaves, flowers and trees. Books and inset jigsaws encourage children to identify everyday shapes.

Geometric shapes have names to distinguish them. Solid or three-dimensional shapes include cubes, cuboids, cylinders, spheres, cones, prisms and ovoids. Plane or two-dimensional shapes include squares, rectangles (with right angles), oblongs (any four-sided figure), triangles and ovals.

When children first identify and name geometric shapes, they often refer to an item that is usually that shape. For example, Caprice called a triangle a 'witch hat'. You may find it helpful to refer to common objects when referring to shape names. It may help children to associate an abstract shape with a concrete object and thereby remember its name.

Experimenting with shapes

Start off by talking with children about the attributes of different shapes. For example, feel the flat faces of a cuboid and its sharp corners. Handle a prism and use it for printing, naming the resulting triangles with their three straight sides. Compare these with the smooth curve of a sphere.

Let the children consider shapes of different sizes, and hold three-dimensional shapes in a variety of positions so that they can see that this changes the viewpoint but not the shape.

A shape walk

Walk around the nursery and outdoor area looking at the shapes of things. To avoid confusion, ask the children to look for just one or two shapes during each walk. You might see rectangles in windows, doors and mats, cuboids in concrete blocks and fencing, circles in wheels, clocks and signs, and spheres in balls.

Matching games

You can use sheets of wallpaper which have repeating patterns to make cards for the children to use in matching games. Cut the patterns and pictures from the wallpaper and stick them on to plain cards, and then cover the cards with sticky-backed plastic to protect them. Then you can play the following games with the children.

• Snap – make cards which each show one of about six different pictures, and encourage the children to match pairs of cards as they are turned.

• Memory – using the same set of cards, position the cards face down and invite the children to turn up two at a time, trying to find matching pairs.

• Dominoes – make a set of cards in which the cards have different shapes or pictures at each end, and let the children place them with matching ends together, as in the traditional game of dominoes.

• Lotto – divide a large card into four or more sections, each one featuring a picture or shape. Make a separate set of cards for the children to match each section.

Using shape

Help children to experience using shapes by giving them a variety of shape-based activities.

• Ask them to identify shapes in the environment.

• Let them make shapes with their bodies during movement sessions.

• Encourage them to make shapes together with other children, for example, when playing ring games.

• Show them how shapes can change using dough and clay. Taking a fixed amount of dough and rolling or squeezing it to change

its shape helps children to understand the conservation of matter. The shape may change but the original quantity of dough remains the same.
• Encourage the children to combine shapes to make other shapes when they are using scrap materials and construction equipment.
• Let them use sorting toys and puzzles to match shapes. Make silhouettes of nursery equipment to help children to match and put away the equipment at tidy-up time.

Construction equipment

Children can combine the geometric shapes of construction toys to make models. Give them a selection of open-ended equipment that offers a variety of shapes and methods of fastening.

The construction area

The construction area encourages children to build with three-dimensional or solid shapes. This gives them the opportunity to turn, combine and view shapes from different angles. Provide a variety of shapes and fastenings, and include plenty of wheels, windows and small figures to add interest to the children's building and imaginative play.

Furniture
• A sturdy open shelf for displaying wooden bricks offering a variety of shapes.
• A unit with deep drawers for small equipment.
• A shelf or low window sill where children can place finished models.

Equipment
• A set of size-related wooden bricks featuring different shapes.
• A set of play figures, both people and animals.
• A layered system such as DUPLO or LEGO, with base plates and wheels.
• Hollow shapes such as Mobilo, including hinges and other moving connections.
• Stickle Bricks – young children find these easy to join and pull apart. Include base plates and wheels.

• A clipboard, pencils and paper for drawing plans and maps.
• Books with pictures of buildings such as bridges and houses.
• Pictures cut from construction equipment brochures, assembled into booklets to stimulate ideas for building.

Using blocks

A set of small and large size-related bricks gives children the opportunity to combine shapes. As they build, children look at the shapes from different angles and different perspectives.

Small bricks help children to balance, tessellate and explore shape. Small figures and vehicles used with the bricks encourage them to think about space when they are making houses and garages to fit the figures.

A set of large blocks encourages children to build houses and vehicles for themselves. This is often a joint venture and leads to an exploration of space, for example, when they need to discover how many children fit inside a house. If another

child comes along, the children will either call out that there is no more room or start building again to enlarge the house!

Scrap materials

Household packets and containers provide a wealth of shapes to use for junk modelling. Look for shapes such as cuboids in cereal packets, cubes in toiletries, cylinders in custard tins, cones in popcorn containers and prisms in chocolate boxes.

In your junk modelling area you will need to provide:
• household packets, containers and lids;
• coloured papers and foil bottle tops;
• natural objects such as feathers, pine cones and shells;
• methods of fixing, for example, PVA adhesive, paste, a stapler, sticky tape, ties, string and paper-clips;
• blunt needles and open-weave fabric, such as binca and hessian, for sewing.
Groups of children can sew rolls, cartons, foil, sweet papers and feathers on to a large piece of fabric. As the children choose, position and fasten the shapes to the appliqué, they will consider shapes and space.

Nets

Scrap materials bring the opportunity to discover the net of a solid or three-dimensional shape. Carefully open out and flatten boxes of different shapes to reveal their nets. Leave them with the other scrap materials to be assembled and used for modelling.

Two and three dimensions

Printing

Printing with the faces of solid shapes allows children to consider plane or two-dimensional shapes. They can also investigate shapes that roll and compare the different faces of the solids. As they print, they will turn and move shapes. Here are some other ideas to offer the children:
• Paint all the faces of a wooden brick or

cereal packet and print with each face. Compare the shapes. Repeat using a different shape.
• Place a sheet of paper in a tray. Cover a ball with paint and roll it over the paper. Also, try printing with a cylinder, comparing the different faces.
• Blow bubbles with a straw in a mixture of washing-up liquid, water and paint. Let the children watch how the spherical bubble shapes build up, and cover them with paper. Look at the circles that have formed on the paper.
• Print with many different man-made and natural objects, such as plastic containers, cotton reels, leaves and feathers.

Two-dimensional shapes

Let children combine two-dimensional shapes to find out which will tessellate. Technically speaking, any shape with depth is three-dimensional, even a piece of paper. However, you need to give children a variety of shapes that they can handle and move.
• Provide commercially available sticky shapes with which to make pictures and patterns.

• Make or buy some shape puzzles to encourage sorting and matching shapes.
• Give children shapes cut from tissue, crêpe paper, foil and fabric to combine.
• Some computer programs enable children to draw or choose shapes to make pictures or patterns.
• Large pieces of fabric or paper cut into triangles, squares and circles help children to discover which shapes are suitable for using as blankets, shawls and circular tablecloths. By folding these pieces of fabric, children will learn some of the attributes of shapes, for example, their angles, curves and number of sides. By folding some shapes in half along the axis of symmetry, they will discover that a circle becomes a semi-circle and a square becomes a rectangle.

Spaces and shapes

Spaces inside

Encourage the children to discover the spaces within shapes.
• Let the children jump inside the solid shapes of hollow outdoor equipment.

• Fill empty boxes of different shapes with cotton reels, shells or small stones. Ask the children to compare the numbers of small objects it takes to fill them.
• Provide a range of buckets and moulds to make sand pies.
• Make ice lollies by filling different shaped moulds or containers with juice and freezing them.
• Put picture labels on equipment drawers and boxes and ask children to put equipment away carefully so that it fits inside.
• Provide cupboards, bags and cases in the role-play area and let the children fill them with other objects.

Spaces outside

Encourage children to discover the spaces outside shapes by covering boxes and containers with paint, paper, fabric, shells, stones, sequins and other decorative materials.

Spatial awareness

As soon as a child starts to move herself and her toys from place to place, she becomes aware of space. She learns which objects are within reach and which are too far away. In a familiar environment such as home or school, children become aware of distance and location. Give them a wide range of activities to explore the space around them.
• They need to discover the space immediately around their bodies. Movement, possibly to music, encourages them to stretch and use the space over, around and beneath them.
• They need to explore the space that they have access to by climbing, crawling, walking and sliding. The space around them can be explored by pushing carts, riding scooters and building with blocks.
• The space above them can be explored by blowing bubbles and flying kites.
• Catching and throwing bean bags and balls helps children to estimate the space between people. Throwing quoits or hoops over upturned bins or skittles helps them to estimate the space between objects.

Making models

Making models with construction equipment or scrap materials involves using shape and space. When children first use building blocks, they begin by experimenting with shape and fastenings, finding shapes that fit together and constructions that balance. They consolidate these discoveries by repeating them. A child who has just learned how to build a bridge may want to repeat this several times before she feels ready to attempt something different. A child who can confidently construct a bridge may

want to build a larger one, or another one the same size but with different shapes. Children gradually acquire a system of making tried and tested buildings which they adapt with increasing confidence.

Children have an idea of what they want to build and what it will look like. They can talk you through their design. As Lara was building she said, 'You go up some stairs and then you're in the house bit. It's a hot air balloon.'

Observing
Watch as children select and reject building materials to achieve their goal. How do they choose and combine the shapes that they use? Look at the shape of the whole construction. Do children experiment with height as they build tall vertical towers? Do they explore length in making long horizontal walls? Do they play with the idea of enclosure by making a building shell? Look for pattern and symmetry in the shapes they use.

Listening
Listen carefully to what children say as they build. They will talk about their design, the choice of materials, what the model represents and its function. They

change their ideas as they go along and depending on availability of materials. What was originally intended as a wall is soon converted into a house. They spot new potential in the construction and make a new plan.

Straight and curved
Linear tracks such as model rail lines and roadways suggest ideas for combining straight and curved lines in different ways. Tracks need not always loop; there are many other ways to combine them. Try making straight, wavy and circular lines. Draw children's attention to the shape of the lines and encourage them to use the spaces around them for positioning figures, buildings and animals.

Let the children assemble the track for themselves. Initially, they will fasten together random pieces of track. Later, they will sort through and select the shape they require.

Offer the children a challenge. Place a tunnel and a station a small distance apart and ask whether the children can assemble the track so that the train goes through the tunnel and to the station. Give them junctions and bridges to offer scope for more complex layouts.

The linear arrangements of tracks and roadways lead naturally on to the idea of plans and maps, which represent three-dimensional shapes using two-dimensional symbols.

Plans and maps

Introduce the idea of a plan view by showing children a two-dimensional view of their three-dimensional construction. You could take photographs of the constructions and models, or draw 'pictures' or plans of them. Display the model alongside its plan or photograph to show the children how the two-dimensional plan represents the three-dimensional model.

Drawing plans

Drawing plans of their constructions helps children to become aware of the use of shape and increases their understanding of spatial relationships. Encourage them to help you draw plans by naming the features to be represented and adding their own representations to the plan.

Children's own plans are usually characterised by an attempt to represent the whole model. This leads to the juxtaposition of a side and an overhead view. They also tend to draw figures and vehicles inside the buildings. This is termed transparency. They often take into account the texture of the construction material. For example, Russell drew the bristles on Stickle Bricks, and Annabelle the notches on LEGO.

The significant differences between children's drawings and their constructions can either be attributed to the importance children attach to specific features, which leads them to draw those features larger, or to their drawing ability.

Plans reveal not only a child's drawing ability and perception but also her concepts of relative size, position, number,

one-to-one correspondence and sequential pattern.

Design briefs

With experience, children can draw a plan of a model they *intend* to construct, as well as representing its final shape. Discuss the plans with them to help focus their ideas.

First designs are usually stylised versions of the objects children want to make – the typical house, car or figure of early drawings. Children then construct their model without looking at the plan. At this stage, an idea is represented in two different ways – by drawing and by modelling.

With more experience, children will draw a design brief and name parts and specify materials. Some intended features may prove unsuitable, and alternatives will be found. The child will realise that the original plan was impractical and will change it. Drawing plans encourages children to do some forward thinking and also reflect on past work.

Introducing maps

Discuss with the children the layouts they have constructed with lengths of rail tracking. Encourage them to use language associated with spatial relationships, such as near, far, close and around.

Standing over a track they have made gives children an aerial view of the layout, which is a prerequisite for understanding maps. There are various other ways of enabling children to get an aerial view of a layout.
• Let them look down at a playmat which has tracks and buildings marked on it.
• Show them aerial photographs of the local area, with landmarks the children will recognise. Most children respond readily to side or oblique views of well-known landmarks, and find that vertical elevations offer more of a challenge.
• Take the children on visits to locations which offer an aerial view, such as a hill or even an upstairs view from the school or another building.

Making maps

Start off by making a map yourself, with help from the children. Invite them to suggest features for your map and add some of their own. Draw large maps and leave them on the floor or table for children to use with small cars and figures. Children will respond to the appropriate sign, for example, stopping the car at the 'garage' for petrol.

When they have got the idea of maps, children will enjoy representing the layouts they have made in map form. At first, children may look intently at the road or rail track they have made but do not consider the appearance of the track on paper. They often exaggerate corners and junctions and may include features which do not exist on the layout but are present in their imagination. Encourage them to devise their own symbols for the map, for example, to indicate the road and buildings.

Early maps

A map is often an indication of how well a child understands the connection between one place and another. As they draw their map, they have to consider distance and location. Children's early attempts often result in pictorial or iconic maps where they indicate the form of objects more clearly than their location. They may use an oblique or side view of objects or buildings.

Early maps are often full of rich individual detail. For example, when Katie drew a map, the landmarks were a supermarket trolley and a house with three steps. Children often show people and vehicles, for example, Gemma drew her baby sister's buggy outside the local supermarket.

The proportion used in children's first maps will often relate to their own experience of the area. For example, a long, weary hill may be exaggerated.

Ideas for maps

You can make maps based on a variety of layouts and environments, including:
• layouts that children have made;
• the nursery, indoors and outdoors;

• areas in the nursery, for example, the role-play area;
• journeys that children have undertaken, particularly the journey from home to school;
• an area close to the nursery which can be visited and discussed;
• imaginary journeys that feature in stories and imaginative play.

Computer toys

Computer toys that can be programmed to move in different directions encourage children to explore spatial relationships and expand their vocabulary. You could try the following ideas.
• Program the vehicle to move forwards, backwards and sideways, and introduce the terms left and right.
• Measure a single unit of distance by marking a card and cutting it to that length. Measure and record a double unit and mark off each unit. Ask the children to estimate how many units the toy will take to reach a brick. Test it. Adjust the estimate and try again.
• Discuss the turns the toy makes. Introduce the idea of a half turn and full turn.
• Draw a map or plan of a course you want the toy to travel along. Use this on another occasion as a basis for estimating how many units and in which direction you will need to make the toy travel.

Your role

• To provide the opportunity to explore three-dimensional and two-dimensional shapes.
• To offer materials for building with shapes.
• To provide materials for making and changing shapes.
• To offer activities for discovering the two-dimensional faces of three-dimensional shapes.
• To provide opportunities to discover spatial relationships including distance and location.

Handling data

Sorting

Sorting is an integral part of early years experience. Let children sort or select items according to a specific criterion which changes on different occasions.

• At tidy-up time, ask the children to sort the equipment and return it to the appropriate area. Picture labels on drawers, containers and shelves will help. Cut out pictures from catalogues or make silhouettes of equipment such as rulers, scissors, crayons and pencils.

• When preparing materials for an activity, encourage children to sort scrap materials brought from home into boxes with picture labels, for example, cardboard rolls, paper, containers and trays. Close-up photographs could also be used as labels.

• Let the children suggest criteria for sorting items on the investigation tables. Items can be sorted by colour, shape or size. For example, children could make sets of items that fit in a specified container. Send children on a search around the nursery looking for relevant items for the table.

• Watch as children play. They will be sorting bricks of a certain size and shape, outfits to wear from the dressing-up trolley and pictures to cut out and stick. Encourage them to talk about what they are choosing and why.

• The children can sort themselves into groups according to different criteria, for example, those with laces, buckles or Velcro on their shoes.

• Encourage children to sort objects or pictures of objects according to criteria, for example, things we need at bath time or kitchen equipment.

Recording

Children's activities and experiences can be recorded in a number of ways:

Talking

Expressing ideas in words is the first and most important form of recording. Encourage children to discuss what they are going to do, predict possible outcomes and talk about what they are doing.

Investigation tables

Provide a means of recording with real objects. An investigation table could provide a range of activities, together with ways of recording results. For example, an exploration into shapes that tessellate could include opportunities to use mosaics and a range of sticky-backed paper shapes. It may feature examples of children's printing with blocks that tessellate. The latter provides a more permanent record of their work.

Representing

Children need a chance to represent or record their experience of objects in dough, clay, painting, modelling, movement and drawing. Remember to praise and encourage the children's work.

Diagrams

Children enjoy making simple block graphs. Offer the children different fruits to taste. After they have tasted two or three fruits, give each child a happy face sticker to place under the picture of their favourite fruit. At the end, count the happy faces and compare the numbers.

Chapter 5
Science

The early years classroom, with its emphasis on first-hand experience, offers a wealth of scientific potential. There are opportunities for scientific investigations within most of the areas of the classroom. Children are investigating as they play with natural materials such as sand, water and clay, and construction materials such as Mobilo, scrap materials and large building blocks. They begin to use machines such as radios, cassette players and televisions, and they can also be introduced to the computer.

During the early years, children undertake themes or topics that broaden their horizons and develop an awareness of the world around them. They can follow up these interests with the investigation tables and activities that their teachers provide, such as growing seeds and using magnets.

There should also be plenty of opportunities to use and explore the outdoor environment, including the garden, and to prepare and taste food, which involves observing changes as ingredients are heated or cooled. All these practical investigations can be backed up with stories and information books about topics which interest the children.

At the end of this chapter there is an example of the sort of chart that could be used for recording children's achievements in science, mathematics and technology.

An enquiring mind

Children who actively seek answers to questions will have a positive attitude to discovery and experimentation. However, not all children are willing to explore and experiment. Some children have not had the opportunity to develop an enquiring mind. As a new nursery teacher, I was astonished to find some parents sending their children through the door with firm instructions, 'And don't get in a mess or play in the paint.' Children need to explore and experiment without worrying; their clothes can be protected with aprons. You may need to discuss this aspect with parents to ensure that they send their children to nursery suitably dressed.

Support children's natural curiosity about their environment by encouraging them to seek answers to their own questions. Ask them more questions to encourage them to explore, and take advantage of events that capture their interest.

Children's questions

Children who are given the opportunity to participate in digging, growing, building and baking observe new aspects of everyday life and want to know more about them. The question 'Why?' indicates an important landmark in children's development. The physical exploration of materials has awakened an intellectual curiosity that seeks and creates explanations. This is one of the cornerstones of science.

It is important to encourage and listen to children's questions and explanations. The reasons they give for phenomena may not be strictly accurate, but they are the result of scientific thinking. Children draw on their previous experience to make causal connections between events. Their questions demonstrate their interest and knowledge. Do not discourage children from experimenting in their own way. For example, one child brought in a pebble from the beach that looked very much like the potatoes we were growing. He planted it beside them and we waited to see what would happen.

Questioning is the key to predicting, testing, observing results and coming to conclusions. These conclusions provide the foundation for more abstract concepts, such as that of gravity.

Questioning children

The way you question children is also important. Science is about enquiry and is a continuous process in which knowledge raises new questions. Closed questions that seek a pre-defined answer do not encourage a child to question and explore. You need to ask questions which help the children to interpret the phenomena they see. For example, when they are observing something, ask, 'Have you seen...?', 'What's happening here?' or 'What is it doing?' When children compare two objects, ask them in which ways they are the same or different. Encourage them to predict results by asking, 'What will happen if we try this?'

Encourage them to give explanations and look for causal links by asking, 'Why do you think that happened?'

Investigating

Using all five senses

First-hand experience of everyday objects, natural materials and events are central to the early years curriculum. Children who observe closely learn about their world. Encourage children to use more than one sense when they observe. Some items, for example, a lemon, can be seen, touched, smelled and tasted. Let the children touch, taste, hear, smell and look at a wide variety of objects and living things.

Touch

Investigation tables can feature a range of surfaces, for example, soft cotton wool, hard wood, furry fabric, rough bark and smooth velvet.

Encourage children to use touch to identify things. Place some objects in a bag or box. Ask the children to put their hands in the bag to feel, describe and guess what the object is. You can make this into a game, encouraging children to take turns.

Encourage children to handle and discuss everyday objects and surfaces as they play, for example, the slide, the sand and water. Make touch part of the investigation when children are considering natural things such as buds, leaves, shells and petals.

Taste and smell

Use food activities to give an opportunity for tasting and smelling. Fruit and vegetables offer a wide variety of scents and tastes: try lemon, orange, apple, celery and spring onion.

Place samples of foods which smell differently, for example, coffee and chocolate, in containers. Ask the children to smell them and guess what they are. Supervise the children while they do this as they may attempt to taste the food.

Let the children smell and taste different food flavours, for example, strawberry and banana. Try making milkshakes, jelly and yoghurt. Ensure that the flavourings and colourings you use are not those associated with hyperactivity; use the actual fruit where possible.

Hearing

Ask the children to listen to sounds made by a variety of objects and animals. Let them shake objects, for example, seed pods, and make noises by scraping a variety of surfaces, such as that of a pine cone.

Make shakers from containers such as yoghurt pots and margarine tubs. Try using shells, gravel, paper clips, sand, bits of plastic and wood inside them to make the sound. Cover the pots with clear acetate film so that children can see the objects making the sounds. Ask them to listen for loud sounds and soft sounds. Create a guessing game with opaque shakers and ask the children to guess what is making the sound.

Ask the children to make different sounds with their voices, for example, whispering, singing and shouting. Let them do the same with their hands, for example, clapping, patting the floor and banging their fists on top of each other. Musical instruments also offer a range of sounds to listen to and explore.

Go on a listening walk. Walk around the school or locality listening out for a variety of sounds. Many sounds are so much part of everyday life that we no longer hear them. Encourage the children to listen for traffic and try to identify individual sounds, for example, a bus, lorry or car. What else can they hear?

Play 'guess the sound'. Make sounds behind a screen with everyday objects and encourage children to guess what you are doing. Try assembling LEGO, stirring a drink in a cup and scraping a bowl with a spoon.

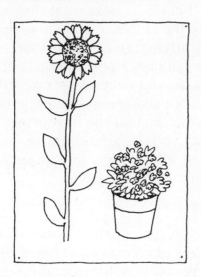

Listen to and discuss with the children commercially-available tapes which feature different sounds. Make your own tapes with the children, using familiar sounds. Groups of children from different sessions can exchange and guess the sounds on each other's tapes.

Sight

Encourage the children to look closely at objects. Ask them to describe colours, shapes and patterns. Point out details like the parts of a flower.

Play 'guess the object'. Ask the children to close their eyes or cover them with a scarf. Place an object in their hands. Can they guess what it is? Not all children like having their eyes covered, so be prepared to take the first turn.

Introduce magnifying glasses and viewers for close observation and leave them on the investigation table. Heavy-duty microscopes will enlarge familiar items, for example, hair, but very young children find it difficult to associate an object with its enlargement. Binoculars are useful outdoors, but they need to be durable.

Resources for science

Investigation tables

Investigation tables are a focal point for exploring, observing and experimenting; they give children a chance to handle and use objects. They may have a specific theme, for example, 'rocks' or 'toys that move'. Inform parents of the theme so that children can contribute items.

Involve children in setting up the tables. Let them select relevant posters and books, as well as objects from different parts of the school or nursery. Discuss other items and where you would find them.

Invite children to make models or draw pictures of the items on the table. Some themes, such as 'spring buds' or 'growing seeds', allow children to observe and monitor changes over a period of time. Put out magnifying glasses and viewing boxes

for close observation, as well as measuring instruments such as balance scales and string.

The contents of the table will increase and change, reflecting the interests of the children. Some themes last for several weeks and become a focus for explorations that take place throughout the nursery.

The food area

The food area gives children a chance to investigate using all five senses. It provides experience with a variety of foods, and children can watch the effects of heating and cooling substances. They can observe changes of state from liquid to solid and vice versa. Introduce them to a range of kitchen tools, and show them how they are used. Let children help with grating, shredding, mixing, mashing, kneading and stirring different ingredients.

Try to provide a choice for them at some stage. For example, would they prefer to make sultana or cheese scones?

Remember, however, that all activities in the food area require supervision.

Equipment

Furniture
• Wipe-clean tables and chairs.
• An oven with a hob.
• A sink.

Tools and resources
• Wipe-clean aprons for you and the children.
• A washing-up bowl reserved for food equipment only.
• Chopping boards.
• Cutlery.
• Mixing bowls in three sizes.
• Standard kitchen scales.
• Non-standard measuring equipment such as cups, bowls and spoons.
• Baking tins and trays.
• Transparent saucepans.
• Assorted tools such as a sieve, a colander, a whisk, a grater, a juice squeezer and a masher.

Ideas for the food area

Yoghurt

Bring one pint of milk to the boil, and remove it from the heat. Leave the milk to cool until it is lukewarm – about blood temperature. Yoghurt thermometers are available, but are not essential – you can do a 'baby's bath' test to ensure that the milk is neither too hot nor too cold. Warmth activates the bacteria that turn the milk into yoghurt, but too much heat kills them.

Pour half the milk into a bowl. Measure two tablespoons of plain live yoghurt, add it to half the milk and stir. Gradually add the remaining milk, stirring well. Pour the mixture into a vacuum flask and leave it overnight or for about nine to twelve hours. When the yoghurt is made, chill it and then offer it to the children to taste. Let them add some fruit to flavour the yoghurt if they wish.

Cream jelly

Take a packet of fruit jelly, and cut the jelly into pieces. Put the pieces in a bowl and pour over 450ml hot water. Stir to melt the jelly. NB: Always take care while using hot water when children are about.

Chill the jelly in the fridge until it is nearly set, and then stir in 150g natural or flavoured yoghurt. Leave the jelly in the fridge until it is fully set, and then let the children taste it.

If you make cream jellies in a range of flavours, you can ask the children to compare the tastes.

Scientific skills

Communication

During observation activities, it is important to let the children describe what they are seeing, hearing, touching, smelling and tasting. Help them to find the appropriate words, but give them enough time to express their own ideas.

Investigating the effects of a magnet on different objects, one child declared, 'Look, it sticks!' Give them the opportunity to:
• describe what they are observing;
• ask questions;
• listen to explanations;
• discuss the experience with other children;

- search for information using different sources, for example, books and visitors with specialist knowledge.

Observational representation

Asking children to look closely at insects or flowers and then draw them is an excellent way of encouraging observation. You may not be able to recognise the drawing but by listening to the children as they talk about what they are drawing or modelling, you will hear some interesting insights into the child's perception of the object.

Observational representation, whether through drawings or models, encourages some useful scientific skills.
- Children observe closely the colour, shape and other details of the object.
- They concentrate on one object for a long period.
- They talk about their observations.
- They record their observations.

Let the children represent what they see in any medium they choose. On fine days, put the easels outside so that children can paint flowers, trees and insects. At times, use powder paint to encourage children to mix colours. Crayons, chalks and felt-tipped pens can also be used very effectively. Chalks are useful for representing pale objects on dark paper.

Give children a chance to do some representational modelling with clay or scrap materials. This will encourage them to consider the form and shape of the object they are observing.

Comparing and classifying

Describing and representing objects encourages children to become aware of their features and attributes. This, in turn, helps them to compare objects and recognise their similarities and differences. Help children to identify features and to make links by matching or comparing objects.

Invite children to sort objects on the investigation table into natural and man-made materials. Encourage them to select items for the table from school or home, which they can then sort according to their own criteria or ones chosen by you. One child made a collection of 'things that see me' or reflective surfaces, including a spoon, a mirror and some foil.

Children enjoy sorting through boxes of random objects speculating on where they came from and what they are. Let the children sort the items under broad headings, for example, objects that roll.

Predicting

As children explore different materials, they start to develop expectations, for example, dry sand flows but wet sand does not. As they repeat activities (often termed 'practice play'), children test their predictions.

When their expectations are confirmed, children begin to reason logically. John declared that water came out of a funnel, 'because it's got a hole in it. See.' John tried other objects with holes and finally he made a hole in a yoghurt pot to test his

theory. A hypothesis had been formed and a new world of possibilities discovered.

Young children's theories are rarely limited to one area. John's 'hole' theory was explored in sand, clay, the construction area and even the home corner. When we made biscuits, John was absorbed in cutting holes of different shapes using pastry cutters. This pattern of purposeful exploration is called a 'schema', and many have been observed in young children's play. However, it is important to observe closely and, if necessary, interact sensitively with individual children as they explore.

Let children predict what may happen in a variety of situations, for example, when using magnets or sowing seeds. Children's predictions are often logical, but not necessarily correct: 'The little seed (an orange pip) is a tiny flower and that big one (a bulb) is a high, high tree up there.'

Children need the opportunity to repeat activities, so make sure resources are available every day. They also need the chance to explore different materials to discover possibilities. Let them plan their own activities to put new theories into practice, and give them access to informed staff who can support or extend their activities and ideas. Equally importantly, children need plenty of encouragement to make and test predictions. This winter we placed a bulb over a transparent container full of water. I explained how roots grow and drink the water. After half-term, the children rushed up excitedly to tell me that the 'white straws' had grown.

Measuring

Encourage children to estimate and measure during the course of activities. Let them compare objects to see which is longer, wider, taller or faster.

The idea of temperature can be introduced by changes in the water tray. Fill it with warm water and let the children note how it cools over time. In winter, fill the water tray with ice or snow and ask the children to monitor changes in temperature. A baking session gives you the chance to show how standard measures of temperature are used on the oven. You can also discuss temperature in relation to our bodies, that is, whether it feels hot or cold. Never let the children be exposed to extreme temperatures.

You can measure forces during outdoor play and when using toys with wheels. Pushing hard on a trolley full of children, or watching as a ball rolls down a gentle slope, allows children experience of forces in a form that can easily be put into words.

130

Your role

• To create a stimulating environment that encourages observation and questions.
• To encourage children to observe, describe, predict and explain.
• To use the potential of daily events, such as mopping up spills, and familiar materials, such as sand and water, as a focus for experimentation.
• To introduce new stimuli to challenge children's interest.
• To be aware of the scientific potential of all areas of the nursery.

Topics and themes

The introduction of a topic or theme allows children to observe and investigate related phenomena. Certain areas of the school or nursery, for example, the sand, water and outdoor areas, are ideal for close investigation. Many of the activities and observations will arise naturally as children play. By observing their play, you can introduce the relevant language and provide further activities to extend their ideas.

There follow some suggestions for open-ended topics which you can adapt to suit the needs and interests of the children in your class. All the topics have a scientific slant, but they can also support work in other areas of the curriculum.

Life and living processes

Topic 1: Ourselves

A topic on 'ourselves' gives opportunities for using the five senses (see pages 125 to 126), and enables you to consider the human life cycle and the children's daily routine, as well as health issues such as food, rest and exercise.

Our bodies

• Turn naming parts of the body into a guessing game, asking, 'Can you find your ankle? Your nose? Your shoulder?'

• Rhymes and songs encourage children to recognise and use parts of the body. There are many appropriate rhymes, for example, 'Heads and shoulders, knees and toes' (in *This Little Puffin* by E. Matterson, Puffin) and 'Ten little fingers' (in *Round and Round the Garden* by Sarah Williams, Oxford University Press).
• Printing with fingers, hands and feet encourages observation and comparison.
• Drawing around hands, feet and the whole body is great fun.
• Show the children how to make impressions of their fingers, feet and hands in dough or clay.
• Let them look in a full-length mirror and note their eye and hair colour. Can they draw themselves as they appear in the mirror?

Differences and similarities

• Ask the children to make sets, for example, 'children with brown eyes' and 'children with black hair'.
• Let the children compare their feet and hand sizes using drawings or prints.
• Compare heights by standing children back to back or in rows in height order.

What our bodies can do

• During outdoor play, let the children practise climbing, balancing, pedalling, pushing and pulling.
• During indoor play, let them sew, paint, draw, build, fasten their coats and put on their shoes.
• Do some movement in a large space, and show children that our bodies can stretch, roll, slide, curl up, sit and lie down. Experiment with different ways of using the feet, to run, walk, tiptoe, shuffle, skip, hop and jump.
• In a smaller space, encourage children to use their hands to wave, clap, pat, stroke, clench and shake. Explore other movements in a similar way, encouraging the children to make suggestions.

Our life cycle

• Display photographs of the children as babies, and photographs of members of their families.
• Invite a family, including grandparents if possible, to visit the nursery. Look for similarities in eye or hair colour and other features.
• Talk with the children about people of different ages – babies, their size and what they can do; toddlers, their size and what they can do; older brothers and sisters and how they spend their day; parents, their size compared to children and what they do; and grandparents, their role in the family.

The pattern of the day

• Read picture books that feature the daily routine.
• Make a book with the children about a typical day, cutting out pictures from magazines to illustrate meal times, school time, bath time, bedtime and so on.
• Ensure that the role-play area has items that are used at different times of the day such as cereal boxes, a lunch box and a dressing-gown. These will help children to act out daily routines.

Healthy living

• Discuss the food we need for growth and health. Let the children sample breakfast cereals and make toast. At lunch time discuss packed lunches and what we eat for lunch.
• Invite the dentist to discuss dental health with the children.
• Personal hygiene is part of every nursery and school routine. Emphasise the importance of washing hands after using the toilet and before food activities. Some children need to be shown how to wash their hands. The importance of washing ourselves and our clothes can be reinforced by caring for the class doll. Place a bar of soap and some baby shampoo near the water tray and leave a towel nearby for children to give the doll a bath. On another occasion, wash the doll's clothes in the water tray with some soap powder. Take children to the launderette to wash clothes from the role-play area.
• At the right time, you can demonstrate the importance of rest and exercise. After demanding physical play, young children are often tired and you may need to invite them to rest quietly and restore their energy. As more children travel in cars and

not all have gardens to play in, the role of exercise is becoming increasingly important. For many, nursery or school provides the main source of physical play. Evaluate children's needs and devise a programme of physical play and movement.

• Safety at home, at school and on the roads needs to be emphasised. The Royal Society for the Prevention of Accidents (RoSPA) has songs and stories which feature road safety. Parents may need information about safety and young children.

Topic 2: Living things

Plants, trees, minibeasts and animals fascinate young children, who can be encouraged to care for them. Let them consider the conditions necessary to sustain life and observe changes over a period as plants and animals grow. Record the changes with observational drawings and photography. Studying the wonders of nature will help children to respect living things and give them a sense of responsibility for their environment.

Help children to realise that all living things are part of our environment. Their habitats must be respected and conserved and if you are out on a walk, for example, you should only allow the children to collect a minimum of specimens. Help them to look after them carefully and later return them to their environment.

During a topic on living things, you can introduce a wide variety of life. Help children to identify living things by showing them large colour photographs, posters or books. It is not easy to observe closely a moving insect, so posters and photographs are useful for showing wing patterns and other small features.

Caring for living things introduces the life cycle of plants, trees and animals. You can also observe how living things respond to seasonal and daily changes. At an early stage, young children start to categorise plants and insects into broad groups, for example, those that crawl.

Encourage children to consider an animal's features, its home, how it moves and what it eats. Compare the similarities and differences with other living things they know. Use story books and non-fiction to complement your topic.

The garden

Outside

• Look for seasonal changes in trees and plants, and in bird and insect life.

• Encourage children to care for living things, for example, by growing seeds, planting trees and feeding birds.

• Go on a minibeast hunt. Make sure that children observe rather than collect them. Turn over stones, look at old walls and behind creeping plants.

• Make minibeast traps by leaving out empty upturned orange and grapefruit halves overnight. Cut a hole in the skins so that the minibeasts can get inside.

• Observe birds. What do they eat in summer? Feed the birds in winter. Sow some birdseed in spring to observe and identify the various shoots that grow.

Inside

• Create a minibeast environment inside a plastic tank so that children can observe the creatures and discuss how they change over time.

• Classify animals according to broad categories such as those that fly. This means that birds, butterflies and ladybirds are in the same category. This is often a source of debate, for example, some children may claim that grasshoppers fly while others decide that they hop.

• Bring in twigs so that children can observe how they change. For example, buds develop into blossom, which falls, and then fruit begins to set.

• Grow bulbs and seeds in the classroom. Let children observe the changes, for example, the hyacinth flowers wither and the seeds set.

Pond life

Before embarking on this topic, make sure that you follow safety rules; consult your LEA guidelines. Some primary schools have a pond which you may be able to visit. Take a large transparent tank and fill it with a bucket of pond water so that children can look at a selection of small pond creatures.

Outside

• Look out for trees and plants that grow in and near the pond.

• Ask the children to watch out for fish and other creatures, for example, frogs, toads, newts, water snails, pondskaters and water boatmen.

Inside

• Set up a freshwater tank with gravel and pondweed. Goldfish and water snails are easy to keep and children can help to look after them.
• Do not collect large amounts of toad and frog spawn. A very small amount may be permissible, but look after it well, keep it for a short time and return it to its environment.

The sea-shore

Check LEA guidelines and tide-tables before making a visit to the sea-shore. An alternative is a visit to a marine life centre where the undersea world is on view.

Outside

• Visit a fish stall to look at the variety of sea life including crabs, whelks, flat fish and other creatures.
• Look for different seaweeds including long oarweeds, bladder-wrack with its air pockets and finer ones such as sea lettuce.
• Look for molluscs such as limpets and winkles on rocks. Observe how tightly they cling.

• Look for other sea-shore creatures such as anemones and starfish.
• Watch the actions of the birds on the sea-shore. They may follow boats and pick up scraps of food left by holiday-makers.
• Observe plants and grasses growing on or near the shore. Look at the sizes and shapes of trees. Many will be bent with the force of the wind.

Inside

• Set up a marine tank with an aerator. Molluscs such as limpets and winkles are easy to keep. Include different types of seaweed. Children will be fascinated to watch anemones opening and closing.
• With the children, make a collection of shells from sea creatures. Name the creatures that they belong to and show the children pictures of them.
• Let the children look at a sea fish such as a cod or plaice. Observe its scales, fins, gills and markings. How do they think it moves in the sea?

Earth and the environment

Topic 1: Litter

A topic on litter can introduce the subject of waste materials and how our activities affect the earth.

Litter outside

• Explain to the children the importance of keeping the school grounds free from litter.
• Ensure that there is a litter bin in an appropriate place.
• Observe how some litter decays, for example, paper, while other litter does not, for example, plastic.
• Sweep up litter in the school or nursery garden.
• Explain the importance of not dropping litter in the street. What do the children think happens to litter on the street? Watch as it blows about on windy days. Observe how the street-cleaning van passes and sweeps up the litter from the edge of the road.

Litter inside

• Keep the nursery free from litter.
• Help the children to make posters asking parents and other visitors to use the litter bin.
• Look at types of packaging in the scrap materials area, for example, cartons, containers, pots, boxes and trays. What are they made from? What did they contain? How can we reuse them?
• Look at packaging in the food area. What sorts of container are used for food? Why? What are the differences between containers that hold liquid, powder or solid substances?
• Ask the children to find out what sort of things get thrown in the nursery bin. What happens to the waste after it reaches the bin? Observe the dustcart collecting rubbish from school.

Recycling

• Ask children and their parents to collect newspapers, boxes, scrap materials and old greetings cards for you to use in the classroom.

• Talk with the children about the amount of packaging that is routinely thrown away. Can they think of any ways of using things that would otherwise be thrown out?
• Many charities can raise money with certain waste materials, such as aluminium cans and waste paper. Invite parents to support a charity in this way, using the school as a collection point.
• Litter is a problem in many communities. Consider with the children the effects that pollution and the disposal of waste have upon the local environment, discussing issues that are relevant to the children, for example, broken glass on the beach or dog waste in the park. Support community efforts to keep the area tidy, and encourage children, staff and parents to take pride in the appearance of their school.

Topic 2: Weather and the seasons

A topic on weather provides the opportunity to describe and record daily changes, as well as seasonal variations. Consider the influence of weather on

aspects of our daily lives, such as children's clothes and games. The length of the day and the passage of the sun over the sky can introduce shadow games and an investigation into sources of light.

Warm and cold

Outside

• Providing children are appropriately dressed, they should have opportunities to play outdoors, experiencing the variety of weather: sun, snow, rain and cloud. How do their clothes help to protect them from the weather?

• Provide outdoor activities that encourage children to consider the weather, for example, water play in summer and snow modelling in winter.

• Encourage children to describe and name the clothes they are wearing and link them to the weather, for example, wearing boots in the rain.

Inside

• Record daily changes in the weather. Make a weather calendar and create symbols for the different types of weather and for the clothes worn, for example, gloves or boots.

• Organise an investigation table to feature the seasons, and ask the children to find appropriate items, for example, spring buds or summer flowers.

• Investigate materials that keep us warm, dry and cool. Start by considering the clothes that children are wearing.

• Fill three small plastic bottles with warm water, tighten the lids, and cover them with materials that children recognise, for example, knitted material, fur fabric and thin cotton. Observe which bottle stays warm the longest.

• Consider the foods we eat in cold weather, for example, soup and toast, and in hot weather, for example, salad and ice-lollies. Make and taste these foods in season.

• Read picture books associated with the weather, for example, *The Wind Blew* by Pat Hutchins (Bodley Head/Puffin). Sing rhymes and devise finger games that feature the weather, for example, 'Rain, rain, go away'.

Sun

Outside

NB: Warn children that it is dangerous to look directly at the sun.

• Play shadow games. Invite children to jump, turn and twist, watching their shadow change. Ask the children to try to lose their shadow. Invite them to stand in the shade of a building or tree and watch how their shadow disappears. Why has it disappeared? Listen to the children's reasoning.

• Look at the shadows cast by familiar objects such as fences, trees and buildings.

• Choose some familiar equipment which children can hold and turn, for example, rackets, hoops and skittles. Ask them to turn these objects and observe the changes in their shadows.

• Watch the passage of the sun. Mark on the play surface with a chalk line the position of the shadow of a young tree or fencepost. Later, return and mark the new position. Do the children know why the shadow has moved? Observe a sundial at different times of day.

• Paint with water. Use paintbrushes of different sizes to draw pictures with water on the play surface. Watch as they evaporate in the sun.

• Look for rainbows after a shower of rain.

• Take the water tray outside, add a little cooking oil and observe the rainbow colours. Add washing-up liquid and agitate the water to cover the surface in bubbles. Let the children observe the rainbow colours on the bubbles. On a sunny day, put some clear water in a transparent water tray and watch the rainbow colours that appear on a nearby surface.

• Take large sheets of coloured acetate film outside and look through them. Ask the children to describe what they see. Include some clear sheets of film and discuss transparency. Look for other clear and coloured transparent objects, for example, lemonade bottles, windows, tumblers and sunglasses.

• Go on a walk to observe colour in the environment. Discuss natural and man-made objects.

Inside

• Look for shadows in the nursery.

• Make shadows using other sources of light, for example a torch or lamp. Heavy duty children's torches with coloured filters are available.

• Look for the rainbow colours that appear as the sun shines through the windows.

• Place sheets of coloured film at child height over the windows. Look through these and discuss colour changes.

• Make 'light beams' with unbreakable mirrors. Reflect the light from the mirror on to a wall or other surface and move the mirror in different directions.

• Fasten a selection of safety reflectors to black paper and shine a torch at them.

Rain

Outside

• Let the children feel the rain on their fingers and faces.

• Look together at the rain forming puddles on pathways, running down drains and soaking into the ground.

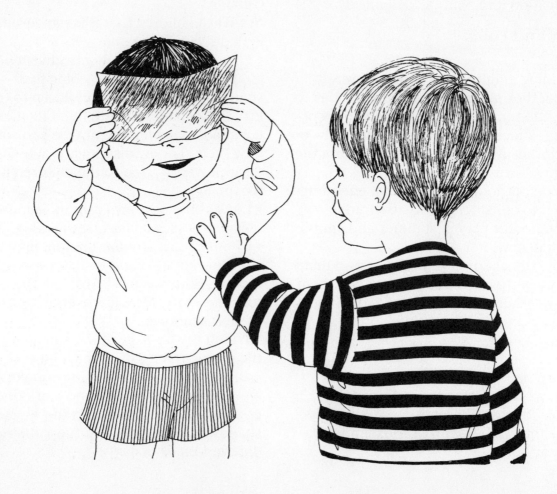

• Observe slugs and worms on the grass and paths.

• Place a bowl outside to catch the rain. Measure this in non-standard units, for example, a bowlful.

• When the weather clears, let the children ride wheeled vehicles through shallow puddles and watch the parallel tracks appear on the play surface.

• Draw chalk lines around the outside of puddles, and come back later when the puddle has reduced in size. Can the children guess what has happened to the water?

Inside

• Describe the rain. Is it a shower or a downpour?

• Let the children use sprays and droppers in the water tray. Ask them to try to pour just one drop, then a succession of single drops and then spray water using a watering can.

• Investigate materials that keep us dry. Make three large cardboard frames. Then cover each frame with a different material, for example, net, cotton and plastic sheeting. Pour water slowly over the materials. Is the material waterproof? Talk with the children about clothes that keep us dry in the rain.

• Let the children mix runny paint and watch as it forms puddles on flat surfaces and runs down the easel.

• Mix a watery paint and let the children make splatter paintings and blobs by gently knocking the end of a brush.

Wind

Outside

• Let the children observe the effect of the wind on leaves, litter and clothing.

• Fly a kite together. Watch how it rises and falls in the wind.

• Give the children a bunch of long streamers or a balloon on a string to hold and see which way the wind is blowing.

• Set a flag in the nursery garden and watch as it blows in different directions.

• Paint the points of the compass on the play surface. Chalk on the direction of the wind. Relate each point of the compass with an identifiable feature, for example, north towards the gate. At first, children find it easier to refer to the direction of the wind as 'blowing towards the door' and rarely use the names of compass points.

• Let the children blow bubbles and watch as they rise and fall.

• Wash the dolls' clothes. Hang some to dry on a washing line outside and leave others inside. Which ones dry first?

Inside

- Design and make a kite to test outside.
- Blow up a balloon, fill another with water and compare the two. Consider shape, weight and contents. Over the water tray, pop each balloon in turn. NB: remove all pieces of balloon immediately.
- Let the children design and make small tissue 'butterflies'. Place them on a floor or table and blow them along.

Snow

Outside

- Let the children make impressions in the snow with the soles of boots and gloved hands.
- Encourage children to make shapes by gathering snow and pressing it together.
- Fill different containers, for example, a bucket and bowl, with snow to make snow pies.
- Encourage everyone to work together to make a snow castle.
- Observe snow: it falls as delicate flakes, is soft and fluffy at first, is hard when pressed together and becomes icy and slushy later.
- Look with the children at the seasonal changes associated with winter. Describe how the snow makes things appear differently and how it affects wildlife.

Inside

- Put snow in a large container, for example, the water tray, for children to explore.
- Place a small amount of snow in two transparent containers. Leave one outside and the other inside. Observe as the snow inside melts. Ask the children to compare the snow in the two containers. Talk about the temperature, for example, one is warmer and the other colder.
- Put water in the freezer to make ice. Place some ice in a transparent container and let the children watch as it melts. If you colour the cubes with food colouring, this makes it easier to observe the water level.
- Replicate footprints made in the snow. Mix paint in a tray and make prints on paper with the soles of unwanted shoes and boots.

Materials and their behaviour

Topic 1: Natural and man-made

Children have access to many different materials throughout the early years. As they manipulate, build and cut materials, children learn about their properties and uses. Make sure you are aware of the potential of the many types of materials in the classroom.

Children need to make many discoveries about materials. They will explore texture, colour, shape and size, and categorise substances by whether they are shiny or dull. Children will find out what they can do with materials, for example, bend, squash, squeeze, cut, tear, sew, see through, break, rejoin and stretch them. They will also consider what things can be used for, for example, pouring, planting, making prints, making moulds, watering seeds or kneading.

Look with the children at the ways materials change, for example, when water is added. Look at the effects of cooling and heating. Do the substances dissolve, melt, solidify or change in other ways? Let the children help you mix powder paint and make dough, watching the changes that take place.

Natural materials

Outside
• Go out with the children and look for natural materials such as soil, stones and rocks. Some natural materials are or used to be alive, such as wood, trees, plants and fruits. Look on the ground for materials which are evidence of living things, such as dropped feathers, bark and cones.
• Talk with the children about clothes that are made of natural materials such as cotton, wool and leather, and discuss whether these materials keep us dry, cool or warm.

Inside
• Give the children plenty of opportunities to play with and explore natural materials such as sand, water and clay. Ask them to describe what they see and feel when using these materials.
• Set up investigation tables to focus on a particular natural material. For example, you could ask the children to find as many different wooden things as they can, and arrange them on the table with books and posters about trees, vases containing twigs, and other items connected with wood.
• Let the children inspect natural materials such as sand and soil through magnifying glasses.

Man-made materials

Outside
• Go out and look for materials used in buildings and vehicles, such as glass and plastic. Look at road surfaces such as Tarmac.
• Talk about clothes that keep us dry, such as boots and raincoats, many of which are made from man-made materials. In wet weather, try out their effectiveness.

Inside
• Let the children use different adhesives, such as paste and PVA, and experiment with paint of different consistencies and on surfaces tilted at different angles.
• Let the children paint on a range of different materials, including absorbent cloth and non-absorbent plastic.
• Let them build with construction kits made of different materials.
• Look around the classroom for examples of materials which are used in different ways, such as glass and plastic.

• Give the children magnifying glasses with which to explore the surfaces of many different materials.

Topic 2: Food

Taste experiences can be classified according to whether food is sweet, sour, salty or bitter. Ask the children to group foods into those they like or dislike and food for growth and health, as well as sorting fruit and vegetables into separate categories.

Taste and smell are closely related. Invite children to consider the texture of food. Is it soft, hard, chewy, crunchy or crisp? Let the children smell foods in the food area. Some have no smell, in particular flour and pastas. Contrast this with the sharp tang of citrus and the warm smell of baking bread and cakes. Encourage children to describe what they can smell and taste.

A topic on food allows you to introduce solids, liquids and gases. Some solids, such as pastry, are kneaded; others, such as cabbage, are shredded, sliced or torn. Liquids, such as water and milk, are used for binding cake mixture, diluting drinks,

blending in soups and reconstituting dried foods. Boiling provides an introduction to gases. Use see-through pans and let the children watch at a safe distance as the water bubbles and boils and the pan fills with steam. Try steaming vegetables.

Demonstrate to the children how substances can change. This can be as a result of heating, for example, custard thickens, vegetables soften and cakes rise. Show them, too, how the effects of heat vary, for example, chocolate melts into a liquid while cake mixture solidifies and becomes firm to touch. Making ice cubes and lollies demonstrates the effect of cooling substances. Emphasise the fact that materials can exist in more than one form.

Introduce the importance of hygiene, setting and maintaining standards. Set a good example yourself, as otherwise children will underestimate the importance of hygiene. Stress the importance of taking care near the cooker and with sharp implements. Before asking children to taste foods, check with parents for any food allergies the children may have.

Health and hygiene

• Discuss the importance of washing hands, wearing special aprons, and making sure that surfaces and equipment are clean.
• Talk with the children about how food is necessary for health and growth. Include a high proportion of savoury dishes when you cook in the classroom, and introduce wholemeal and other flours.

Properties of food

• Describe the sight, smell, touch and taste of food. Let the children listen to the sound of grating and stirring, and the crackle of crisp food as it snaps, for example, pasta and celery.
• Encourage the children to sort food into groups, for example, fruits, seeds, food from stems such as celery and from roots such as carrots.
• Measure with standard and non-standard units while you are cooking. Discuss with the children ways of measuring time, weight, volume and capacity.

Changes

• Look at changes in substance, for example, egg white when raw is transparent; when whisked, it becomes white and peaked, and when it is cooked, it becomes pale brown and hard.
• Show the children the effects of heat, for example, butter turns to oil and biscuits harden.
• Show them the effects of cooling, for example, jelly sets and chocolate hardens.
• Look at what happens when you add water, for example, pasta swells and sugar dissolves.
• Look at materials which exist in more than one state, for example, granulated sugar, icing sugar, castor sugar and syrup.
• Show the children what happens when you use tools, for example, whisks, graters and juice squeezers.
• Provide an element of choice, for example, let the children decide whether to add cinnamon or sultanas to an apple pie.

Topic 3: Water

Water is an ideal substance to investigate, both inside and outside the classroom. Encourage the children to classify materials according to whether they sink or

float, absorb water or are waterproof. Include small figures, water animals and boats to encourage imaginative play.

Water outside

• Talk about where water comes from, and the different forms it takes – clouds, rain, snow and ice.
• Watch where water goes as it soaks into the ground, flows down drains, and forms puddles. Talk about how it finally flows to the rivers and seas.
• Discuss and try out some of the uses of water; watering plants, sailing boats, swimming, paddling, washing cars and windows.
• Visit a zoo to see plants and animals that live in fresh and salt water, for example, ducks, beavers, seals and penguins.

Water inside

Measuring

• Measure with standard units. Provide graded bottles, jugs and other containers based on a litre.
• Measure with non-standard units. Include cups, spoons such as a teaspoon, dessert spoon and ladle, as well as lids and containers of varying sizes and shapes.

The five senses

• Touch: let the children feel some warm and cold water, and add ice so they can feel it when it is very cold. Add washing-up liquid to the water and agitate it to make bubbles. Let the children feel the bubbles and fill containers with them. They could blow bubbles through rings of wire.
• Smelling: add perfume, peppermint or lemon essence and bath salts to water.
• Sight: add colourings and bubbles to the water or leave it clear. Ask the children to look at the surface to see whether it is rough, smooth or wavy. Let them make ripples in rings or V-shapes, swirl the water with their hands and whisk it with a handwhisk. Add a spoonful of cooking oil and observe the colours on a sunny day. Place pebbles and stones in the water and watch how they change colour and seem shiny.

• Sound: listen to drops of water falling, the sound of a water jet and water sprinkling through a spray. Let the children blow bubbles in water with straws and tubing.
• Taste: give the children drinks, jellies, lollies and soup to taste. How do these compare with the taste of plain water?

The properties of water
• It makes things wet; use aprons to protect clothes!
• Water takes the shape of its container; provide transparent containers of different shapes and sizes for the children to fill with coloured water and observe this. Let them try filling and emptying a transparent polythene glove with coloured water.
• Water runs downward; provide jugs, teapots and containers with lips for pouring. Ask children to observe as water runs through their fingers. Provide transparent tubing and funnels to enable them to watch water flow. Let them investigate siphoning water with a tube.
• Water flows over surfaces; provide flat sheets of plastic to observe how water spreads and flows.
• It can be contained; provide containers of various shapes and sizes, for example, lids and buckets.
• It finds its own level; coloured water and transparent containers will demonstrate this. Look at different levels in the water tray. Encourage children to help empty the water tray.

• Water runs through holes; provide sieves, bottles with holes at different levels, flower pots and colanders. Also, give the children objects with many large holes and some with one small hole at different levels.
• Water dissolves certain substances, such as bath crystals or powder paint. The children could also try using powdered foods in the food area, such as sorbet mixes or dried mashed potato.
• Water changes some materials, for example, shells and stones become shiny while fabric becomes darker and more limp.

Water and materials
• Some materials absorb water; provide sponges, flannels and towelling to show this. Try testing different materials for mopping under the water tray, for example, newspaper, polythene, a towel and a tissue. Let the children use different materials for wiping their hands, for example, a paper towel, a sheet of paper, a piece of netting and a towel. Which one is best?
• Some materials are waterproof, such as aprons, raincoats, umbrellas and boots. Let the children test a woollen glove and a rubber glove by putting them on and immersing their hands in water. (This test is not always reliable as some rubber gloves mysteriously fill with water!)
• Some materials float; include cork, wood, large beads, straws and lolly sticks in the water tray.

• Some materials sink; include stones, acorns and shells. Children can see the effects better with a transparent water tray.

The uses of water
• Try using different containers to test which is the most effective for watering plants and seeds.
• Use water wheels, pumps such as hand-cream containers, jets such as washing up liquid containers and sprays such as a watering can. Let the children use these to explore how water's force can be used.
• Talk about how we use water to wash ourselves. Discuss hygiene routines.
• Place some dolls' clothes in the water tray for the children to wash.
• Put a doll in the water tray with soap, flannel and shampoo.
• Let the children watch a baby being bathed.
• In the food area, make orange and other flavoured squashes, and let the children watch you make tea and coffee. NB: keep all hot liquids away from children's reach.

Technology
• In the scrap materials area, design and make something that floats, and test it in the water tray. Make changes if necessary.
• Acquire some plastic guttering that fits together easily and leave it in the water tray for children to explore. Include bends and corners.
• Give children the chance to develop skills in using equipment effectively, for example, jugs, funnels and tubing.

Topic 4: Sand

Sand can be used both wet and dry. Let the children add water to dry sand and observe the changes in colour, texture and weight. Give them small figures, animals and vehicles to encourage imaginative play.

Sand outside
• A large outdoor sandpit is excellent for co-operative exploration and building.
• Visit the sea-shore, if possible, to examine creatures and plants that live on the sand.

• Let the children look at beach sand through a magnifying viewer to see pieces of shell, stone and other materials.

Sand inside
Measures
• Weight: before the children check the weight with a balance scale, let them hold two containers, one full of sand and one empty, and compare their weight.
• Volume and capacity: provide a variety of containers with regular and irregular shapes. These can produce some interesting results. Make a sand pie with a yoghurt pot which has a raised base and stand the pot next to it. Discuss volume and capacity with the children.
• Non-standard measures: include lids, pots, spoons and cups for measuring out quantities of sand.
• Standard measures: include graded bottles and containers of various shapes, for example, bottles, cylinders and cubes, which each hold one litre.

Dry sand
Dry sand is similar to water in the way it can be poured and sieved.
• Sand finds its own level; provide containers of different shapes for the children to fill and empty. Containers with hollow handles and appendages are particularly interesting.
• It flows downward; provide sand wheels, jugs and other containers from which to pour sand. Let the children try using funnels and tubing.
• Sand takes the shape of the container; let the children try containers of various sizes and shapes.
• It runs through holes; include sieves, flour shakers, flower pots and colanders. Mix gravel or shells with the sand to see what will run through and what cannot.

Wet sand
• Wet sand can be moulded; include buckets, graded containers and moulds, and encourage children to use their hands to mould shapes. Let them make impressions in the sand with shells, pine

cones and scrap materials. They can make patterns with their fingers, sand combs and rakes.
• Holes can be made in wet sand using spades, spoons, scoops, shells and containers.

Topic 5: Clay and dough

Clay and dough are modelling materials that can be stretched, squeezed, separated and rejoined without causing any damage. For modelling, clay needs to roll and bend easily without cracking. Damp it periodically with a sponge or cloth, as it dries out at room temperature. Let the children work with wet clay and watch as it dries, to observe how the material changes.

Properties of clay and dough

• Modelling materials can be smoothed by patting them with the fingers or rolling with cylinders.
• They change shape when squeezed, pounded or pressed. Let the children experiment freely with this.

• Clay and dough can be moulded into flat, round or irregular shapes. Strips can be wound together. Let the children use dough of different colours and watch how the shades blend together.
• Clay and dough can be broken and separated with the fingers or with implements such as clay tools and spatulas. They can be rejoined by pressing, kneading or squeezing them together.
• Let the children make impressions in clay and dough by pressing leaves, shells and other objects into the material. Look closely at the intricate surface patterns left in the clay. Patterns can also be made using fingers or tools.

Equipment

• Help the children to use equipment such as clay tools, cutters and rolling pins.
• Encourage the children to weigh clay and dough using balance scales. They can weigh the material using standard weights or non-standard ones such as blocks or toys.
• Process modelling materials to change them. Dry out clay items that children have made, and bake dough objects in the oven at a very low heat until they are hard.

Energy

Topic 1: Toys

Exploring and constructing toys can introduce children to forces and electricity. Discuss and investigate toys throughout the early years classroom, as well as toys from home. Encourage children to make their own moving toys, either using construction equipment with moving parts or scrap materials.

As children investigate commercially-available toys, let them examine what toys can do, for example, roll, bounce, float or move in different directions. Encourage them to think about what we do to toys to make them move, for example, push them, pull them, pedal them, wind them up, switch them on or blow them.

Explore sources of energy, for example, magnets, electricity and gravity. Don't forget the power of our own bodies!

Toys that move

Outside

• Let the children push and pull toys with wheels, for example, wheelbarrows, buggies, scooters and trolleys. Investigate starting, stopping and moving

• Look at pedals, for example, those on bikes. Investigate rotation and momentum. Emphasise the importance of riding safely so that no one is injured. Introduce a 'highway code' to ensure the safety of children in the playground, for example, riding in one direction to avoid collisions. Make signs that indicate a few simple rules. Discuss safety on the roads and the importance of holding an adult's hand when crossing the road.

• Consider weight and gravity in relation to balancing toys, for example, a see-saw or a rocking boat. Investigate what happens as different children take turns.

• Use different types of balls, for example, airflow, sponge balls and footballs, and compare the way they fall and bounce. Hoops and beanbags provide further experience of gravity in action.

• Using a slide, investigate slopes. Place a strong plank horizontally on the ground. Compare moving along the horizontal plank with moving down the slide.

• Investigate flight, using balloons, bubbles, kites and simple paper planes.

• Let the children move about on climbing frames and other large equipment. Where does their energy come from? Discuss food for growth and energy.

• Make toys with sets of blocks, planks and other large construction equipment. You could try making see-saws, slides, slopes and bridges.

Inside

• Investigate toys with wheels. Place small vehicles in different areas of the classroom, including the large block area, and in wet and dry sand to investigate gravity, friction and rotation.

• Include wheels and axles in the construction equipment and scrap materials. Provide circles of strong card to fit over dowelling.

• Investigate slopes. Set up a slope in the nursery and challenge children to find or make something that rolls. In my nursery, one child cut pieces of plastic and placed these inside two margarine tubs that were then taped together. As the toy rolled down the slope, it rattled.

• Let the children use standard construction equipment to make a wheeled vehicle. This is quite a challenge as children need to place the wheels so that they rotate in the same direction, and they must also fix them far enough away from the chassis to enable the model to roll. Other children may choose cylindrical bricks or cardboard rolls. The challenge encourages children to hypothesise, test and evaluate their findings. Introduce them to comparative measures, saying, for example, that one object rolls faster than another. Lower the plank until they find the level at which models no longer roll.

• Investigate toys that float and sink. There are various toys that depend on floating or sinking to move, for example, diving frogs that slowly fill with water. Challenge children to make small sailing boats that move over water. Let them agitate the water or blow the boat.

• Encourage children to make or find something that floats. Plastic trays and margarine tubs are useful. Children will enjoy this activity. Some will be eager to repair boats that sink while others will use them for imaginative play, creating a rescue mission using small plastic figures.

• Use wind-up or clockwork toys. These are fascinating for children. Make tracks to see how far vehicles or figures travel before they need winding again. What happens when the children wind the key?

• LEGO provides wheels that turn after winding a key, and they can be attached to any model. Compare the speed of a model travelling up a slope and one travelling down.

• Some toys, such as fishing games and train carriages, rely on magnets. Encourage children to investigate which parts connect and whether they can find anything else that is attracted to the magnet.

• Use magnets to make a toy. Ask the children to paint a biscuit tin lid. Give them some small commercially-available magnetic strips and ask them to attach them to the back of some pieces of coloured card. Let the children use the lid to make patterns or faces with the card shapes.

• Investigate toys that need batteries, for instance, the computer toy that moves over the classroom floor. Take out the batteries and program the toy. Ask the children why it does not move. Replace the batteries. Ask how we know when the batteries need recharging. Do the children know how we recharge batteries? Demonstrate a recharger and how it is plugged into the mains. NB: do not leave the recharger within children's reach, and always warn them of the dangers of electricity. Sockets

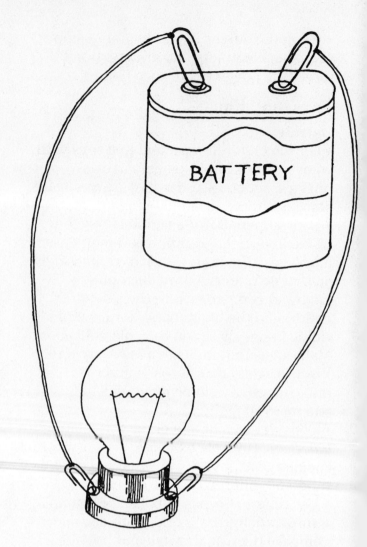

in the nursery should have safety covers when not in use.

• Make a simple circuit to light up a model that children have made. This will require a low voltage battery, a bulb and holders, wire and paper clips. Make sure that you never use a battery that has a higher voltage than the bulb to which it is linked.

Topic 2: Machines

Introduce science and technology through the investigation of machines used at home and in school. It is important that children recognise which machines use electricity and learn that misuse is dangerous. Let them carefully examine the parts of a machine, identifying what they do and how each part relates to the whole system. Children also learn about the function of machines as they use them. Let them investigate what the machine is used for, its function, and how it works.

148

Information technology is a means of communication used for storing and sending messages. As children help to send messages for a purpose, they begin to appreciate the function and diversity of the machines. Let the children watch you working with machines and give them the opportunity to use them under your supervision. Demonstrate a cassette recorder to show children exactly what it is used for. Let the children record their voice and listen to the tape. You can then send this to someone and ask them to reply to the children by recording on the tape. Although this will show the children what a tape recorder is used for, they will not necessarily understand how it works.

Vehicles

Create a garage for 'repairing' wheeled toys. Set the toy to be mended on a raised surface or table, perhaps turning it upside down. This will help children to consider a familiar toy in a new light. Discuss the parts and how they relate. Consider a scooter, a wooden vehicle, a bicycle and other toys with wheels. NB: supervise children to ensure that they do not trap their fingers in any moving parts.

Household equipment

• The food area is a valuable source of machines and tools that children can use, for example, a whisk, a juice squeezer and a grater. Introduce unusual tools, for example, a garlic press or a butter curler.
• Encourage children to participate in using machines in the nursery as they are required, for example, the washing machine, the vacuum cleaner, the oven and the fridge. Discuss why each machine is required. NB: ensure that children are not exposed to danger and warn them of the potential dangers of household equipment.

Communications

• Record songs and messages on a cassette tape for children in another class. In a part-time nursery, the morning session could send a message to the afternoon children. Let the receivers respond in a similar way,

otherwise the children may feel that their message has 'disappeared'.
• Make a cassette with different children speaking or saying rhymes. Play it in the listening centre for children to guess which of their friends is speaking.
• Use a video camera to film the children playing. Show it to the children and to the parents.
• Listen to music, stories and songs on the radio. Children are usually more accustomed to the television, so start with short extracts.
• Television programmes can enhance children's understanding of a theme, for example, watching a variety of creatures hatch from eggs. Talk about the programmes after you have watched them.
• Many children arrive at school familiar with a computer, while others may never have used one. Integrate the use of the computer into the early years curriculum. The most suitable programs for early years are open-ended, developing problem-solving and language skills. Before using a program, consider the clarity of the graphics, the size of the type, the pace of the program and whether or not you can change it.
• Create letters or messages for friends and parents using a word processor. Put up a noticeboard in the writing centre to display them.
• Telephone volunteer parents and let the children speak to them.
• Draw pictures and messages and photocopy them to give to grandparents and friends.
• Visit the school office to watch the secretary receiving and sending messages by telephone, fax and word processor. Watch the postman deliver the post at school, and take the school letters to a nearby post box.
• Write and post a letter inviting someone from the ambulance or police services to visit the nursery. Ask if they can demonstrate a two-way radio. How does the vehicle communicate to other road users that there is an emergency? Let the children watch the lights and listen to the sirens on vehicles.

MATHS, SCIENCE AND TECHNOLOGY

CAROLINE MATUSIAK

- Enjoys using a computer.
- Enjoys observing and has used a magnifying glass.
- Willing to talk about what s/he is doing, seeing, hearing, touching, tasting and smelling.
- Willing to guess what might happen and test it.
- Chooses sand play. Experiments with wet and dry sand.
- Chooses food area
- Willing to explore and experiment activities
- Has a caring attitude to others and the world.
- Has planted seeds and watched them grow.
- Enjoys looking after plants, animals and insects.
- Can plan and complete an activity.
- Chooses water play. Experiments e.g. floating, sinking, displacement etc.
- Enjoys using clay and dough.
- Asks questions, especially why?
- Enjoys taking part in school activities.
- Willing to record through modelling painting, movement etc.
- Can describe parts of the body.
- Willing to work with others
- Repeats activity to see if it happens again.
- Concentrates or chosen activity.
- Enjoys taking part in household activities.
- Makes patterns with bricks, beads boxes etc.
- Has experienced measuring for height, weight and length.
- Chooses to sort and match objects with a common feature.
- Writes number of objects to 5 1. Picture 2. Tally 3. Number
- Names shapes including:
- Knows a number rhyme
- Counts to 5 1 Matching 1-to-1 2 Uses number names
- Enjoys physical play. climbing, balancing, running, hopping and wheeled toys.
- Can replace equipment and geometric blocks on to their silhouettes.
- Chooses construction. Makes towers, walls and houses. Makes appropriate use of wheels.
- Uses the word 'because' and reasons why.
- Knows that money is used when shopping
- Names colours including:
- Chooses junk modelling and uses materials of a variety of shape, size and texture.
- Enjoys problem solving.
- Can relate photos and pictures to real objects.
- Enjoys fitting things together and taking them apart.
- Talks about position, speed and direction.
- Knows that clocks and watches mark time.
- Describes how things are the same / different
- Willing to tidy up and replace objects where they belong.

Chapter 6
Foundation subjects

The foundations for many subjects, including art, music, history and geography, are laid during the early years. These are an integral and vital component of nursery activities, and help to provide a broad and balanced curriculum. Doing and learning are closely interwoven, and skills learned through experience with technology, art, physical education and the other foundation subjects have a wide relevance.

It is play that links together the different areas of the early years curriculum. As a child designs and builds a house or vehicle with large blocks or crates in the role-play area, she is engaging in maths (using shapes), science (investigating forces), and technology (creating an environment). Discussing this enterprise with others and subsequently taking on roles is the focus for work in English (speaking and listening). The addition of relevant literacy

Technology

'The two essential elements of technology that ought to feature in the curriculum in the early years are designing and making activities. Wherever possible children should be encouraged to respond creatively to design problems and develop an interest in improving what they have made.' (DES *Starting With Quality* [The Rumbold Report], HMSO 1990.)

Young children have a natural interest in finding out how things work, and also in creating their own models. Machines are part of their everyday life and you can draw their attention to how they are used. Technology is closely related to the scientific investigation of materials and their uses. Introduce technology in context in the nursery and home, where its function is easy to identify.

Technology can be approached and applied in many subject-based areas including maths, science, art and music. It provides activities that develop skills such as problem-solving, planning, concentrating, decision-making and evaluating. It encourages children to consider the aesthetic qualities of their own work and that of others as they describe textures, colours and form.

Large-scale technology projects encourage children to plan and work as a team, listening to each others' ideas and trying them out. Parents also need to be informed and involved in their children's model-making so that they can appreciate the effort and perseverance that is required.

Let children explore how information technology is used and participate in the use of machines. They will gradually recognise the importance of existing technology and look forward to using it in the future.

Investigating

Children are attracted to artefacts or objects, and systems or sets of objects that

materials, such as a pad and telephone directory, encourages reading and writing. Taking an overhead photo or drawing a plan of this environment introduces geographical skills. Relating the sequence of activities provides a link with history.

Meaningful situations that contain the elements of many subjects are the essence of early years education. You determine the subject areas as you intervene and use resources to extend and develop young children's ideas. The chart on page 176 can be used to record children's achievements in history, geography, art and music.

operate together, for example, a bicycle. As children play with equipment, they investigate how it works.

Exploring artefacts

• Look together at commercially-available toys that can be taken apart and fitted together, for example, vehicles and clocks.
• Explore construction equipment that can be taken apart and fitted together in many different ways. It is important to include a variety of moving parts such as cogs, wheels and hinges.
• Provide a range of real objects that are safe for children to look inside to observe working parts, for example, an alarm clock with a ringing bell. Children will quite happily dismantle anything, and they need to know which objects are suitable and available for this. Set aside a special table or area for taking objects apart so that any misunderstanding is avoided.
• Show the children some household and other machines that can be used under supervision. Introduce a computer, a cooker, a microwave oven, an electronic keyboard and other musical instruments.

Exploring materials

Give children a variety of materials so that they can explore their properties, including texture, hardness, pliability and colour. As they work with them, discuss the qualities of materials and how easy it is to bend or cut them.

Sources of materials

• The scrap materials area. Encourage parents to keep a carrier bag by their kitchen bin to save useful, clean materials including paper, foil, cardboard, lolly sticks, netting, bread tags, bottle tops and jar lids, bag twists, paper bags, wool, fabric and reels. Each season brings a fresh range of materials, for example, you may receive party poppers, streamers, cards and wrapping paper after Christmas and other celebrations. Include fastening materials such as wool, tape, paper clips, paste and a

stapler. At first, children may discover materials that tear easily, or use a lot of paste to stick a tiny item. In this way they build up skills with equipment and knowledge of materials which is applied when they design and make their own models.
• Natural materials. Sand, water, clay and dough should be available daily so that children can explore their properties and use them for making models. Water encourages children to investigate objects that sink or float, and materials that are waterproof or absorbent.
• Construction equipment such as Mobilo, LEGO, DUPLO and Brio Mec. Ensure that children have access to construction kits made from different materials, for example, wood and plastic.
• Woodwork. A work bench with sandpaper is useful for children to explore the properties of wood, cork and other scrap materials. Make sure all activities are supervised.
• The food area. Grating, shredding, squeezing, mixing, kneading and heating ingredients draws children's attention to the different types of food and their characteristics.

Exploring tools

Children need to learn to use tools appropriately, efficiently and safely. Each area of the classroom has tools and equipment that will develop children's manipulative skills and encourage their creativity. Give young children plenty of opportunity to use their hands and build up a range of fine motor movements. For example, let them use:
• scrap materials with scissors, paste brushes, glue spreaders, a stapler, paper clips and paint brushes;
• wood with a pin hammer, sandpaper, screwdriver and hand drill;
• natural materials with clay tools, containers that pour or can be used for moulding in sand or water;
• food with graters, whisks and other kitchen equipment.

Processes

At first, young children explore materials by cutting or bending them; some may simply select some materials to feel, fold and squeeze. Materials may be placed on top of, inside or beside each other. Let the children explore at their own pace and in their own way. Discuss the names, properties, and colours of materials they choose and draw their attention to the similarities and differences between materials.

Later, children use their experience of materials to combine materials for a purpose. They may not necessarily try to reproduce a specific object. Observing them and discussing their creations may be the only way to determine what they are trying to achieve.

What to look for

• A construction that does something, for example, 'This one opens up.' This remark referred to a paper lid that opened and closed.
• A construction that has certain attributes. One child said, 'It's got spots all over,' which referred to a combination of bottle tops and felt-tipped pen marks on a cereal box.
• A nameless construction, similar to one made with wooden bricks, can demonstrate how children develop different skills, including balance, or discover the use of paste to fasten materials. They may say, 'Look how high it is.'
• Patterns, sometimes symmetrical. Children may describe a pattern, perhaps saying, 'It goes round and round.'

Representing

Sometimes you can only determine what a child is representing by talking with him about the model or scene.

What to look for

• Models which change from one thing to another as they are being created. At times this is a process of discovery for the child, who may decide what the model or drawing is by virtue of what it looks like to them, perhaps saying, 'I've made a big blue sea.'
• Models that are personal to the child but which you cannot identify. The child readily explains the parts and their function.
• At an advanced stage, children design and make both real and imaginary objects and scenes, for example, 'It's a goatgruff bridge and that makes trolls trip and fall down, down.'

Designing and making

It is important to encourage children to plan their own models. To a child who is not yet able to represent, models you suggest may simply be 'boxes'.

Planning their own models encourages children to solve problems, select and test materials and explore the types and uses of materials. Encourage parents to work alongside children so that they can see how much concentration, thinking and manipulative skill are involved.

When children have explored materials and forms of representation, offer them open-ended challenges, for example, making something that floats. Leave the choice of subject, materials and fastenings to the child. However, be ready to assist children to achieve their goals. At a more advanced stage, suggest to children that they draw a design brief of what they will make. At first, this may be a stylised version of a vehicle or house. Later, children will draw a detailed design brief and try to implement it. Talking to them will reveal that they realise that certain

parts are not included in the final model, possibly because of a lack of space. They may also point out new parts that have been added.

Large-scale projects encourage children to plan and work together. Large building blocks for use inside or outside encourage children to make their own imaginative play equipment. This has a limitless variety of uses from 'swimming pools' to 'roundabouts'. As children build, they create an environment, considering the systems and artefacts required.

Information technology

Show children how information technology is applied in daily life and encourage them to use it. Show them how a radio cassette is used or let them watch the school secretary use a telephone, a typewriter, word processor or photocopier. Make a telephone call with the children to a volunteer parent, and type a message that they can send through the post or by fax.

Draw children's attention to the control of machines, for example, cookers. Also, emphasise the dangers of machines and electricity. They will be able to use some machines, such as computer toys, for themselves. Ensure that girls and boys have equal access to computers and computer toys.

Provide telephones and other machines for role-play in the office and home corner. See pages 86 to 88 and 120 for more information on the use of computers, computer toys and word processors.

Your role

• To provide a variety of materials and tools for children to explore.
• To encourage children to design and make their own models.
• To support children to achieve their goals.
• To respect whatever the child has been working on.
• To encourage children to discuss what they are doing and using.

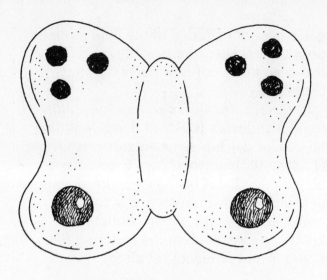

• To introduce information technology, encouraging children to use it and explore its function through imaginative play.

Art
Exploring and representing

'Art, craft, design, music, dance and drama promote the development of young children's imagination and their ability to use media and materials creatively and to begin to appreciate beauty and fitness for a purpose.'
(DES, *Starting With Quality* [The Rumbold Report], HMSO 1990.)

Young children need the opportunity to create their own work and consider that of others. Give them a variety of materials to encourage two- and three-dimensional work. Let them look at and consider the work of their peers and of established artists. Ask them to consider how design is used in the environment, on fabrics, furniture and other items, and discuss whether it is suitable for the purpose. This aspect introduces the links between art and technology. The two are closely associated as children use paint, scrap materials and clay. Emphasis should rest on the creation rather than the end product. Observe how children become totally absorbed in painting, modelling or manipulating clay.

Provide young children with sources of inspiration by introducing them to interesting experiences, natural and man-made objects, and attractive surroundings. By looking closely at objects in order to represent them, children create mental images that can be expressed in a variety of materials. Art is both an emotional and an intellectual response to sensory experience.

On one occasion, butterflies visiting a buddleia bush provided inspiration for the children in my nursery. The children noted the different colours and patterns, and consulted a photographic chart to match the butterflies, asking staff to read their names. Pattern became a fascination. 'Butterflies' were cut from fabrics, torn from tissue and crepe paper which was then painted on one side and folded together, and modelled in two colours of modelling dough. 'Butterfly' biscuits were baked and iced. There was a selection of decorations, for example, glace cherries and currants, from which the children made a pattern and repeated it on the other half of the biscuit. Considering the patterns on butterflies encouraged the children to look more closely at other patterns, such as those on cushions, curtains and clothes.

Representation

Given the opportunities to imagine or pretend in all areas of the nursery, children will develop symbolism or the ability to use one thing to stand for another. At first, young children simply explore art materials. They observe the effects of thick splashes of paint, and watch as thin paint runs downwards or forms pools. Many are satisfied simply to handle boxes and other scrap materials, examining their shape and form, discovering surfaces that combine easily. The pile of boxes or splashes of paint previously designated 'for Mummy', although seemingly unchanged, suddenly becomes 'a boat' or 'a robot'.

A child's ability to represent is a significant stage in abstraction. Parents need to recognise the importance of listening to what children say about their work, rather than demanding something 'nice' to take home.

There are three stages in representation. The first is exploration, where the children explore a variety of media. Secondly, they make personal symbols which are not readily identifiable to anyone other than the child. A picture or model may represent something else as the drawing or modelling proceeds. The third stage is representation, when the model or drawing is identifiable, usually after discussion with the child.

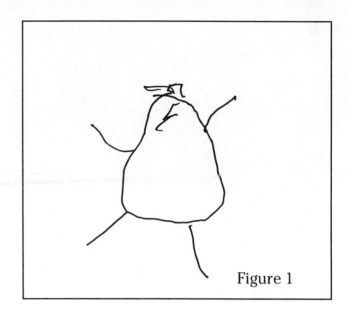

Figure 1

Young children's drawing

Young children need to know that their work is valued. A verbal response and a wish to display the work shows how much you appreciate it. A knowledge of the development of children's drawing will help you to appreciate their work.

Young children's drawings and paintings reflect their intellectual and emotional development. They also demonstrate a search for visual order in the patterns and symmetry of the drawing.

Characteristics

• Children rarely use the bottom of the page as the ground or baseline. They use space as they want to and figures may float in an upright, upturned or slanting position.
• Children do not consider the overall appearance of the picture, but consider each figure or shape in isolation. The picture may, therefore, be composed of several individual units that stand next to each other.
• Children develop a basic figure or shape that they adapt to serve many purposes, for example, they may add more legs for a spider. They invent new figures based on known shapes, for example, a small figure may indicate a baby.
• The basic figure often takes the form of a central circle with lines radiating from it (see Figure 1). These lines may represent

arms, legs, a trunk, ears or hair. At a later stage, another circle may be added for the body. By listening to children as they draw, you will understand what they are representing.

Types of drawing

It is important for children to develop figures and patterns. Patterns may be based on lines, shapes or splodges. There are four main types of painting or drawing.
• Lines. These may explore the possibilities of mark-making. They may also be a deliberate linear sequence. Look for different ways of making lines, for example, straight, zigzag and spiral. A single drawing may include a wide range of styles or just repeat one style.
• Splodges of colour. A child may use a single colour to cover the whole paper or paint several splodges in a variety of colours. Look for sequences and patterns.
• A figure. This may be repeated in other colours or sizes. As children become adept, they will alter these shapes to create houses and animals.
• A shape, for example, crossed lines, dots or a circle. This may be repeated in different or similar colours to form a decorative pattern.

Paper of different shapes and sizes will encourage children to respond to the shape. Some children use circular paper for the face or body while others draw a figure inside it.

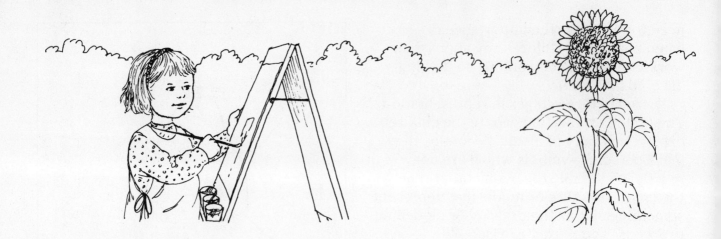

Observing

Provide magnifying glasses to allow children to look closely at a wide range of natural and man-made items. This will help them to develop an awareness of and sensitivity to the environment. Using all their senses helps children to form mental images of the objects they want to represent. Painting and modelling specific items encourages them to perceive and visualise these things as they concentrate on the form, shape and line.

Each child creates a personal representation of an object. Last autumn, I put our easels outside by the sunflowers, and asked the children each to draw one. Each child's sunflower was different. The paintings reflected the child's ability at mark-making, and also revealed his personal observations. Later discussion revealed the individual emphasis on seeds, petals, stalk or even visiting insects.

Ideas for observation

• Encourage children to observe and discuss items on the investigation table, such as shells, growing seeds, rocks, stones, minibeasts, fruit and vegetables.
• Place the easels outside in fine weather close to an interesting object.
• Give children clipboards with paper and crayons. Invite them to focus on one aspect of the outdoor area, for example, a tree.
• Give children the opportunity to record by using movement as well as chalks, crayons, paint and modelling. For example,

they might pretend to be a seed which is curled up and slowly growing.
• Give children time to observe closely and discuss objects. Listen as they talk about certain aspects of the object that they are drawing. Write their words down as a caption for their work.
• In a large sand-pit, encourage children to make patterns and pictures with gravel, shells and stones.

Collecting

Ask the children to help you build up collections of objects and pictures to inspire their artwork.
• Make a group collage based on a subject, for example, teddy bears. This could include pictures cut out of magazines, postcards and greetings cards, as well as photographs of the children's teddies. Extend this into a collection of teddy bears: children's own teddies, old teddies, painted ones, pottery teddies and bears in stories such as Paddington. Encourage children to draw, paint and model teddies for the collection.
• Many children have a particular interest and they could use this as the basis for their individual collection.
• Give children a scrap book which they can use for sticking cuttings and other items of interest. At first, it may be a selection of unconnected pictures that the child likes. Later, children may collect more specific items, for example, toys or birthday cards.

The language of art

Young children need to learn words associated with art so that they can discuss their own work and that of others. As children create their own work, introduce the terms for materials, techniques and colours. Introduce children to paintings, pottery and photographs by artists. Give them a variety of illustrated books that will show them different styles and techniques to enrich their aesthetic awareness.

Attractive surroundings which contain both natural and man-made objects, for example, shells, flowers, wood, plastic, pottery and pictures, heighten young children's perception and provide a stimulus for their own artwork. Consider fabrics and furnishings such as curtains and cushions. Collect familiar objects such as postcards, stamps and sweatshirts so that the children can observe their variety and compare them. Give them a selection of greetings cards to discuss.

Materials and processes

Encourage children to observe and discuss materials and processes as they explore a variety of tools and techniques.

Ideas

Paint

Use powder paint, runny paint with water, thick paint with paste, paint and water mixed with oil to create a marbled effect, paint, water and PVA adhesive with sand or other tiny items added, and powder paint sprinkled onto a watery background.

In summer, let the children paint with water outside on different surfaces and watch as the water evaporates.

Try making bubble prints by adding washing-up liquid to a watery paint solution and blowing through a straw to make coloured bubbles. Place a piece of paper over the bubbles to make a print.

Tools for painting

Use fingers, brushes of different thickness (from fine ones to decorating brushes), string, ropes and threads, toothbrushes, combs, sponges, wheels, straws for blow-painting, and paste spreaders.

Mark-making

Let the children make marks with wax and pencil crayons, charcoal, chalks and water-soluble crayons. Let them make a wax relief

by drawing a picture in crayon and then painting over it. Ask them to try making marks using a twig or finger in thick paint and in wet sand. Encourage children to explore making lines with their fingers on a paint-covered surface.

Surfaces

Use different surfaces for painting and mark-making: rough, smooth, shiny, patterned, embossed and corrugated surfaces. Try making impressions of the raised surfaces of coins, bark and LEGO boards. Tape thin paper over the surface, use a wax crayon on its side and rub gently over the raised surface. Encourage children to look for patterns.

Modelling materials

Let the children use clay, dough, wet sand and scrap materials. Also, introduce them to papier mâché. Give them newspaper to tear into shreds and place these in a mixture of wallpaper paste and water. (NB: ensure that the paste does not contain fungicide.) Show them how to make simple shapes by screwing sheets of newspaper

together. Cover these with the papier mâché. Leave the models to dry, and then paint them.

Collage and appliqué

Use two- and three-dimensional materials such as fabrics, paper (including tissue and card), boxes, tubes, foil and natural materials such as shells and feathers. For collage work, use PVA adhesive. For appliqué, sew the items together with wool, strings and other threads. Use blunt needles and knot the wool at the needle end to prevent the needle unthreading with every stitch. Show the children how to pinch the material and push the needle through for a straight stitch. Encourage them to explore sewing by crossing, looping and oversewing stitches. Ask them to feel and compare the different textures of the threads they use.

I found that a large piece of hessian placed on a table top provided the opportunity for a group of children to sew with wool. Some chose to thread bottle tops and then sew these on to the hessian. Others chose to attach coloured paper and

cotton reels. The result was a colourful and attractive wall-hanging. A caption informed parents about how children tackled the project.

Mixing colours

Provide pots of powder paint, a palette, water and a brush for children to explore colour mixing. Ask them to try out their colours on a separate sheet of paper. At first, children are fascinated by the changing shades and are not interested in using the paint to make pictures.

Give children different shades of tissue paper to stick on to a white or plain background. Encourage them to overlap the shades and observe the colour changes.

Provide coloured acetate film to stick on to a clear or plain background. Again, invite children to overlap the pieces of film to create new colours. Hang the end results against a window for a stained-glass effect or hang them as a mobile near a source of light.

Individual and group work

Children need to work on individual and group projects. Encourage them to plan and complete their work by giving them sufficient time. Make space to store work that can be returned to on a future occasion.

Individual projects

Encourage children to plan their own work and to select an appropriate medium. Help them to achieve their goal by encouraging them to sample many different media and materials. Displaying work allows children to appreciate what they and their friends have created.

Group projects

Encourage children to work co-operatively on projects, for example, making backgrounds for display, large box models, collage and appliqué. Cover display boards with plain paper and invite the children to paint pictures on them to create a colourful mural. Incorporate children's ideas as the work progresses and offer choices for the group to consider.

Your role

• To encourage children to observe and record their environment in two and three dimensions, for example, through painting and modelling.
• To encourage children to visualise and represent objects and experiences from memory.
• To encourage children to develop an imaginative response.
• To provide a variety of media and materials for children to explore and enjoy.
• To encourage children to talk about their own work and the work of others.
• To develop children's awareness of art and design in the environment.
• To value and appreciate young children's art.

Music

Listening and responding

Young children enjoy singing and making music, taking pleasure from the creativity music allows. They also enjoy the opportunity to sing and make music as a group. Introduce them to a wide range of songs and instruments, and give opportunities to listen, join in and experiment. You do not have to have any special musical knowledge to do this. Let children explore music-making and invent their own songs and notation in the same way that they explore the skills of writing and reading. This can be done in a music corner with commercially-available and home-made instruments.

Let the children listen to live and taped music. Listening to music produces a variety of emotions which the children can later express in movement, modelling or paint. Children often try to express their emotions in music and this is reflected in the songs they request and the sounds they make with instruments. Children gradually build up a repertoire of songs and rhymes that helps them to discriminate sounds. There are many potential sources of musical activity in the early years classroom:

• the music corner, where child-made and conventional instruments are available;
• songs, rhymes and finger games with individuals and groups;
• the listening centre, or a tape recorder with headphones and cassettes of songs and music, including recordings of your children singing their favourite songs;
• music and movement sessions;
• keyboards;
• computer software.

Encouraging listening and responding

Everyday sounds

• Create an awareness of everyday sounds in the environment by taking the children on 'listening walks' around the school and grounds.
• Play commercially-available tapes of everyday and more unusual sounds to encourage children to listen to and identify sounds. You can also make your own tapes of sounds in the children's immediate environment.
• Put up a small screen and make sounds behind it using everyday objects. Ask the children to guess what is making the sound.

Songs and music

Encourage the children to listen to and sing a variety of songs and music. This may be done as a group or on an individual basis. One child, who was very withdrawn, joined in eagerly with songs and rhymes. The feeling of being part of a group gave him the security he needed to express himself. Invite older children to sing songs to the whole group.
• Place different types of music in the listening centre, including children's songs, folk and modern songs, and classical and

modern music. Include some tapes of the children singing their favourite songs.

Musical instruments

• Invite older children to talk about instruments and play them for the children. Many are only too willing to learn an additional tune which allows the children to join in and sing.
• If you have some simple instruments in the classroom, encourage children to experiment with the sounds they make.

Characteristics of music

• Introduce the children to the main characteristics of music, for example, pitch (high/low), pace (fast/slow) and dynamics (loud/quiet).
• Explore pitch through stories, for example, 'Goldilocks and the Three Bears'. Allocate a different pitch level to each bear. Play the sound on an instrument when the corresponding bear features in the story. Afterwards, play the sounds on their own and invite children to guess which bear each represents.
• Explore pace through stories, for example, tap out rhythms to indicate the slow or fast footsteps of characters.
• Explore rhythm with the children by clapping in time to songs and rhymes.

Movement to music

• Encourage children to respond to music with their bodies. Give them adequate opportunity to develop their own response.
• Use stories and rhymes as a framework for movement.
• Choose themes with contrasting elements, for example, toys such as light, bouncy balloons and heavy, floppy, soft ragdolls.
• Use music that evokes different moods or emotional responses.
• Play musical games, for example, musical statues.

Making music

There are plenty of ways of encouraging the children to explore sounds and music.
• Let the children experiment with sounds from a variety of sources, including commercially-available instruments and ones the children have made themselves (see page 164).
• Sing a variety of songs, both traditional and new, leading the songs yourself until the children have the confidence to sing on their own.
• Accompany songs with different instruments, perhaps using shakers the children have made.

- Encourage children to hold instruments appropriately and effectively.
- Encourage children to make up their own songs and music. Some children may want to record them or perform them for others.
- Children who know about musical notation will invent their own form of notation, which will reflect early mark-making. Place books and music sheets with words and music in the music corner. This will encourage the children to 'read' and play the music. Some will invent their own system of recording music while others will draw strings of notes which they may ask you to 'play'.

Making instruments

- Try placing elastic bands of different thicknesses over a variety of containers, for example, a vegetable tray, a margarine tub and a yoghurt pot. Pluck the bands. Which one has the clearest sounds? Why?
- Make 'drums' using biscuit and other tins. Compare these with cartons. Tap them with fingers and then with a stick.
- Make shakers (see Chapter 5, pages 125 to 126).
- Set up a class band. Play the instruments to visiting parents and other classes.

Your role

- To foster a love of music.
- To provide opportunities for children to listen to, participate in and make songs and music.
- To introduce the shared experience of music.
- To encourage children to respond to music in a variety of ways.

Physical education

Confidence and control

☞ 'Learning by doing and moving is crucial to the physical, intellectual, emotional and social development of young children.' (*Curriculum Matters 16: Physical Education from 5 to 16*, HMSO 1989.)

All young children need access to equipment, apparatus and space suitable for vigorous movement, such as running and climbing. Regular activity plays an important part in promoting healthy growth; it helps to develop a child's bones, muscles and internal organs such as the heart and lungs.

Give children a range of quality experiences that present a physical challenge.

Physical activity also makes intellectual demands. Children use their judgement, imagination and capacity for problem-solving as they plan and carry out movements. Through practice, they co-ordinate and refine perceptual and motor skills. By learning about and controlling their bodies in relation to space, objects and other people, children realise their physical limitations and capabilities.

When planning physical activities for children, it is essential to take safety precautions into account. Select equipment that has no sharp edges or moving parts which might trap fingers. Safe surfaces offer the best protection against falls. For details, check with LEA guidelines. Check all equipment regularly. Encourage children to plan how to use equipment but ensure that they do not endanger others, themselves or the equipment. Some children are not too confident in their approach to physical play and will need opportunities to use equipment at a quiet time, setting their own targets, however small, to gain some confidence.

Create opportunities for physical play inside and outside the nursery. Informal play, such as climbing, balancing and swinging, needs to be carefully structured to ensure that the equipment encourages a variety of skills. You can also devise formal, teacher-directed activities, for example, games, obstacle courses and dance, but let the children use their initiative as they participate.

Confidence

Children's ability to develop their physical skills depends on confidence and awareness.
• They need the confidence to perform. Encourage children to participate at their own level and pace. Help them to meet their own targets and realise their limitations. Young children need to develop a spirit of challenge in order to explore their potential for movement.

• Children also need body awareness. The awareness of the self in relation to space, to other people and to objects enriches a child's language, perception, cognition and social development. Draw children's attention to what their body is doing and where it is moving. Let them appreciate movement and stillness. At appropriate points, introduce the language of spatial relationships, the names of body parts, movements and equipment.

Physical competence

Equipment such as climbing frames, planks, stepping stones and mats encourage activities such as climbing, sliding and balancing. A versatile system of crates, barrels, ladders and planks encourages children to organise their own use of equipment.

A wide variety of movement experiences will help children to develop essential physical skills. Children need to know about the equipment and the different ways it may be used. For example, children may

discover that a tunnel can be used for going round, on top, along the side and through. Encourage a safe and appropriate use of equipment. Children need to preserve their own safety and that of others, and to care for equipment. They also need the ability to work alone or with others. Social skills such as taking turns and sharing are an important part of this.

Physical control

Young children respond to movement with their whole body. Watch, for example, how a child throws a ball. In the early stages of physical control, the body moves as a unit. This is often termed gross motor control. Later, control over the separate parts of the body increases and this is termed fine motor control.

Give children a wide range of physical challenges to develop a variety of movement patterns. Equipment and activities should offer simple and complex challenges to meet the needs and abilities of all children.

Encourage children to develop gross motor skills as they catch, throw and grip. Introduce them to small apparatus such as balls and quoits. These skills are refined by activities such as threading, mark-making and using small construction toys. These activities also develop hand-eye co-ordination, which is necessary for them to use tools and equipment efficiently, as well as laying the foundations for writing and reading.

In developing these skills, children need the opportunity to explore the ways in which they can move.

The self in space

Asking children to find a space and move from one space to another encourages them to think about themselves in relation to other people and other positions. Encourage them to move in different directions, for example, forwards, sideways, backwards, upwards, downwards and turning. One sunny day, after looking at dandelion clocks blowing in the wind, the children were encouraged to put their arms out to whirl and turn like dandelion clocks on the breeze.

Some activities encourage the co-ordination of perception and movement. For example, when catching balls the child has to estimate speed and distance, as well as assume the correct body position. These activities also encourage an awareness of others. Children need to judge the situation before deciding when, how and where to move. Ensure that they follow simple rules for everyone's safety.

The body as a means of expression

Children need to learn first to move in response to sounds and then to communicate feelings through movement. Movement and dance sessions allow children to respond with their whole bodies to feelings, ideas, stories or music.

Moving and thinking

Familiarise yourself with children's early movement patterns, for example, how children run, throw and catch, so that you can encourage them to make efficient and smooth movements appropriate to their stage of development.

Emphasis should lie in the quality of movement control rather than in performance. Children should develop a smooth running action rather than trying to run as fast as possible. Encourage them to acquire and refine movement patterns.

• Describe the movement they should make, for example, skipping with high knees or walking with long steps. In this way, children are given simple criteria against which they can judge their own performance. This also extends their knowledge of possible movements.

• Playing games gives children the opportunity to practise skills and compare their performance in an enjoyable way. The emphasis at this stage is on co-operating rather than competing. Children watch each other to acquire more ideas rather than to imitate. Simple games such as throwing hoops over a cone or tossing bean bags into a basket encourage children to judge their own performance. Encourage them to compete against themselves, saying, 'That's more than you managed last time', rather than comparing them with others, which can be demoralising.

• As children participate in physical activities, draw their attention to changes in their bodies, for example, when they exercise they breathe faster and become hot. Encourage them to rest after vigorous activity.

Resources

The outdoor area

The outdoor area should provide a variety of physical challenges for informal exploration, enabling children to determine where, when and how to move. If possible, provide a safe surface and a grassed area incorporating paths, gentle slopes, a hill and hollow.

Trees and plants provide shade and an interesting environment in which to explore living things. When planning the outdoor area, take into account opportunities for solitary and co-operative play.

Equipment

Provide equipment that is safe and versatile, offering simple and complex challenges.

• Include equipment made from different materials, for example, wood, plastic and rope.

• Provide a range of different surfaces to explore, for example, soft, hard and grassed.

• Make available equipment with different planes including horizontal, vertical and sloping.

• If possible, equipment should offer different heights and levels for children to climb on.

• Encourage different ways of moving including climbing, crawling, jumping and swinging.

• Equipment should encourage the exploration of forces, for example, a slide and wheeled toys.

• Provide some equipment that encourages balance, for example, beams and stepping stones or logs.

The active area

Children require an enclosed space away from traffic where vigorous physical activity can take place. Make a large space available for ring games and running. Include equipment and space for developing gross motor skills, for instance, a climbing frame, balancing planks, a slide, toys to push and pull, a barrel, strong crates, steps, mats, balls of different sizes, hoops, quoits and bats. Give children the opportunity to use their upper body strength by gripping and hanging. Consider children with special needs. For example, a wheelbarrow encourages hemiplegic children, who have limited use of an arm and leg on one side of the body, to use both hands. Arrange an obstacle course with a variety of skills required at each stage.

A quiet area

Children require an area where they can be quiet, a place where they can observe the world around them. Provide seats, a blanket and large boxes for imaginative play, and sand, possibly in an old tractor tyre. This will need to be covered when not in use. A row of mats encourages children to find different ways of moving, for example, crawling, rolling and slithering.

Invite children to use the garden for growing seeds, looking at plants and watching insects. Provide garden tools and magnifying glasses for close observation. In winter they can feed the birds, while in summer, easels for chalking and painting can be taken outside. The water tray can also be taken outside in summer.

Your role

• To provide a variety of challenging physical experiences both inside and outside the nursery.
• To offer the support and assistance required for children to gain confidence and realise their physical potential.
• To encourage children to consider their own safety and that of others, by following simple rules.
• To encourage children to explore and refine gross and fine motor skills by using the body as a whole, as well as parts of the body.
• To provide opportunities for moving in response to music, stories and other stimuli.
• To understand the stages of physical development and to encourage and support children as they acquire and practise efficient patterns of movement.
• To inform parents of opportunities to involve their child in sports activities in the local community, for example, swimming sessions, gym clubs and dance centres.

Geography

People and places

Visiting places and meeting people is essential if young children are to understand the concepts of geography. By going to different places, they develop an awareness of their surroundings, and observe and identify local features. They will see how space and buildings are used, for example, space might be a park or a building site, and a building might be a school or a post office. Meeting people who work or use local facilities allows children to relate different types of activity to particular places.

Use the outside area to give children experience of seasonal weather changes and of their effect on people and living things. Let children investigate the elements, soil, rocks and water, as these are part of the environment.

Encourage close observation with magnifying viewers to explore the components of soil and sand. The changing weather and seasons give you the chance to explain how different forms of water, including ice, snow, rain, mist and flowing streams, affect people's lives.

At the appropriate times, introduce geographical terms and the language of spatial relationships. Playing with bricks gives children experience in using shape and space, but you can intervene with relevant language. Programming computer toys, building layouts and using playmats will encourage children to consider direction, journeys and modes of travel. Role-play with large vehicles encourages them to put on 'seat belts', consult maps, trace a finger along route lines, and talk about distance and location, 'You go left hand right on the corner. We're going to York.' By doing this, children can explore the roles of people at work and their reasons for travel.

Sources of geographical experience

• Visits to familiar and unfamiliar places.
• Meeting nursery visitors and visiting people at work. The visit of the post person challenged the gender concepts of our children as they referred to her as 'the postman lady'.
• Stories, such as 'Little Red Riding Hood' or *Rosie's Walk* by Pat Hutchins (Bodley Head/Picture Puffin), which include a journey.
• Role-play in which children explore the roles of people in the community. For example, in our nursery in which several children come from fishing families, we made a large fishing boat from a box and invited parents to contribute relevant items. We were given pieces of fishing net, lobster pots and fish crates. The children expertly manoeuvred the nets, steered the boat and unloaded the crates. They taught us about the craft of fishing.
• Imaginative play with small vehicles and figures on layouts with tracks or roadways. Children have an 'overhead' view when they play with such layouts. This perspective is important for map-making, which is primarily concerned with the relationship between places.

• Pictorial playmats with figures and vehicles. These are maps that children use with three-dimensional symbols – that is, vehicles and buildings. Children find it easier to interpret a side or oblique view.
• Stories that encourage children to consider different environments, for example, the seaside, the park and the town.

A sense of place

Children need to build up a mental image or map of their environment. You can help this by:
• visiting the vicinity of the school or nursery, identifying and naming landmarks as you walk;
• encouraging children to talk about and draw their journey from home to school;
• teaching them their address;
• teaching them the names of streets and buildings nearby;
• talking about places nearby, for example, where friends or relatives live;
• looking with the children at photographs of places in the vicinity and identifying them.

Help the children to identify and name streets, buildings and parks, and discuss their uses. Discuss similarities and differences between buildings and areas.

Encourage children to talk about places they have visited nearby or on holiday. Some story and information books depict life and people in other lands, but choose them carefully as they should offer children a realistic picture of the places.

Inform parents that you are discussing other places and provide a noticeboard for postcards and other pictorial souvenirs.

Collect postcards and holiday snaps in a viewing folder. Write the children's names on the back so that they can be returned.

People and environments

Encourage children to link activities with specific places such as shops and parks.

Meeting people at work.

• When visiting places, discuss the jobs of people the children meet.
• Invite visitors to talk about their work, including parents, other school staff and people who work in public services.

Homes

Draw children's attention to different types of housing. Tackle this sensitively so that no child feels inferior.
• Take a local walk and look out for flats, bungalows and houses.
• Look at holiday photographs of caravans, hotels, tents and boats.

Reasons for travel

From a safe distance, watch the different vehicles that pass the nursery. Name them in turn and discuss their use, for example, to carry goods. Can the children guess where they might be going to?

Encourage children to discuss:
• the journey from home to nursery;
• other journeys they have undertaken and why;
• why service vehicles, for example, fire engines, need to travel.

Role-play opportunities

• Invite the children to imagine they are using different types of transport, for example, buses, ambulances, space shuttles and boats.
• Set up a large vehicle made from boxes. Include maps, suitcases and shopping bags. Let the children decide whether it is a car, bus or ambulance.

Our environment

The school or nursery

• Investigate soil, rocks and water. Make collections of rocks and pebbles for children to sort. Why do they think pebbles are smooth?
• Discuss seasonal changes in the weather and their effects on the children's lives, for example, the clothes they wear and the games they play. Sing songs and rhymes about the weather. Record the weather daily on a weather chart.

Other places

• Look at everyday materials that are used at school, for example, food, and discuss what they are made of and where they come from.
• Consider places that children like and why. These are usually holiday places and leisure parks, but there are always some surprises, for example, fast food restaurants or a friend's house. Places are usually associated with people or events.

Our changing world

• What is being built nearby, and why? What has been demolished, and why? Has any familiar local space changed its use, for example, waste ground turning into a supermarket or car-park?
• Visit any new building in the area.

• Observe any structural changes to the school.
• Let children change their own environment by making a minibeast garden, or plant trees or bulbs.
• Give children an opportunity to create landscapes in a large sand pit, using figures, animals and vehicles. Children can mould hollows and slopes. In this way they can form hills, mountains and valleys. You might suggest that they develop a community, for example, a farm or a town.

Geographical skills

Encourage children to develop geographical skills in a context that is meaningful and that reflects their interests. For example, talk with the children about people and places when visiting places or using layouts.

Observation

Ask questions to encourage children to think about locations. For example, when out on a visit, ask, 'What can we see?' and encourage the children to name buildings and geographical features they know. You can also ask, 'Where are we?' in relation to a familiar landmark that they can see.

Other suitable questions include the following:
• What is this place/building called?
• What is this place used for?
• Who lives or works here?
• How do they travel here?
• Are there any signs of change, for example, new buildings or a change in the use of established buildings? Perhaps the local shop now loans videos.
• Does it look attractive?

Together with the children, observe places, people at work, buildings and their uses, as well as the weather and its effects. Encourage children to identify features, noting similarities and differences.

Following directions

Let the children explore spatial relationships by playing games, making models and arranging layouts. Introduce games which use the language of spatial relationships. For example, give the children instructions to follow such as, 'Put your hand on top of your head', 'Put it under your chin', 'Put it behind your back', and so on.

Graphicacy

Give children practice in extracting information from pictures and signs. Introduce the use of graphics, which are part of the modern environment. Toy and sweet manufacturers recognise the ability of young children to interpret graphics in the advertising and promotion of their goods. An ability to interpret signs, labels and logos lays the foundation for later map work.

Ideas for encouraging skills

Signs and logos

• Display signs in the various areas of the classroom, for example, 'Sand', 'Paint' and 'Food area'.
• Encourage children to interpret logos on packaging in the scrap materials area.
• Draw children's attention to signs in the environment and discuss how they are used and what they mean.

• Encourage children to make signs and labels as they play in the role-play area or when creating layouts.

Plans

• Provide playmats which give children a natural overhead view.
• Take photographs of children's layouts from overhead.
• Make silhouettes of bricks and equipment from different angles. Use them for matching and sorting equipment.
• Encourage children to make plans and maps of models and layouts (see pages 118 to 120).

Following a route

• Place large-scale maps that you have made on the floor or table for use with small cars and figures. Make the maps with the children so that they can suggest and contribute different features.
• Devise a route for the children to follow on a playmat.
• Make a large frieze showing the route of a story character, for example, Rosie the hen's walk around the farmyard in *Rosie's Walk* by Pat Hutchins (Bodley Head/Puffin).

Using maps

Use maps with the children for purposes that they understand. Make large-scale maps of the nursery both inside and out, featuring landmarks that are relevant to the children, for example, the sand-pit. Refer to these maps when children are in the area, and again afterwards to discuss what happened and where.

Use a map of the outside area when walking in the grounds. Recently, we made an autumn trail, collecting leaves, seeds and other seasonal signs. One of each was taped to the map at the place it was found.

Last summer, we collected some minibeasts from the outside area. We drew pictures of the minibeast on the map to indicate where it was found so that it could be replaced in its habitat.

My present nursery is part-time, which means that each group can hide a toy or storybook with a message attached for the other group, marking its position on a map of the nursery. The other group then consults the map to recognise the location and find the message.

Identifying geographical features

• Show the children pictures and photographs of features such as hills, ponds, woods and the sea. Encourage them to point these out in story books and on playmats.
• Provide a selection of travel brochures that depict a variety of landscapes.
• Make a collection of postcards and booklets from holidays.
• Acquire some photographs of oblique aerial views, preferably of the local area so that children can identify local landmarks. Many children relate their personal association with local places; 'That's where my Uncle Bill has his boat', and 'We took the bus to town and Gemma fell down there!'

Representing places

• Go with the children to take photographs of the nursery and other places.
• Encourage children to make models of places with bricks, scrap materials and construction equipment.
• Give the children opportunities to draw pictures of places including home, school and the park.
• Make maps of layouts, as well as maps from memory of short journeys.

Your role

• To provide opportunities for exploring spatial relationships.
• To encourage an awareness of the local environment.
• To help children create a mental image or map of the local area.
• To introduce geographical terms and the language of spatial relationships.
• To encourage children to represent places.

History

History introduces the child to her cultural heritage and provides an insight into current issues. You can encourage an awareness of times past and changes that have taken place by emphasising human achievement. Contrast images of today with images of the past.

There are three points regarding children's development that need careful consideration.
• Children operate in the here and now, so that even yesterday may seem 'years' away. The use of the term, 'a long time ago' prompted a child in my nursery to comment, 'What, when I was three?'
• Children are still working out the difference between fantasy and reality. Factual stories about people and places that are not part of a child's experience may seem fabulous and unreal. Equally, some imaginative tales strike a very real chord of emotion in young children.

• Children learn through first-hand experiences. However, our picture of the past depends upon an imaginative re-creation of people and events. Remember that children are actively engaged in discovering the world around them.

A sense of time

Encourage children to develop a sense of time through many of the activities associated with maths (see pages 107 to 108). Ask children to predict and anticipate a future event, for example, a visit or visitor, and to recall it afterwards. This helps children to:
• label time – tomorrow, yesterday, today, names of days of the week;
• contrast now with then – what they are doing today and what they were doing yesterday;
• sequence time by recalling and describing events in order.

Ideas

• Take photos at intervals throughout visits or special events. Put them in a book to use as discussion points or stick them on separate cards for children to sequence.
• Create a nursery year book with photos of different events in chronological order.
• Make a collection of items that remind children of shared events, for example, a cup from a picnic, a shell from the beach and a sticker from a visiting dentist. Play 'Do you remember?' with the items, encouraging children to recall the events.
• Display photos of the children and staff as babies.
• Encourage the children to draw, paint or make models of events they have enjoyed. There will be a personal selection of detail recorded. 'My mummy was there and she had my teddy. S'got blue ears', Stephanie said as she painted her version of the Teddy Bears' Picnic. Another child painted the food she ate. Listen to what children say as they paint and model.

Fact and fantasy

Give children access to their own culture by using stories about popular characters such as 'The Snowman' by Raymond Briggs (Picture Puffin). Books, such as those written by Shirley Hughes and Janet and Allan Ahlberg, often depict familiar aspects of children's daily lives. Together with information books, these help children to differentiate between fantasy and reality.

Stories in the form of folk tales, myth and legend contain much information about the lives of previous generations. They have survived because of their inherent appeal. Read to the children modern adaptations of stories, information books and stories of popular heroes, as well as traditional folk tales. Provide props in the role-play area for children to act out familiar tales.

Sources of history

People, places and things

• Encourage visitors, possibly grandparents, to bring in photographs of themselves as children. It would also be interesting to see any objects, such as toys or household equipment, that they have kept. Let the children compare the equipment with its modern equivalents. Look for differences as well as similarities. What does it look like now? How does it work? What is it made from?
• Perhaps there are older parts of the nursery or old houses nearby. Point these out to the children during a local walk.
• Provide items that children can relate to, such as old clothes and toys.

Your role

• To introduce children to modern society.
• To develop children's sense of time, encouraging them to recall and sequence events in their own lives.
• To introduce children's culture and heritage in a way that is relevant to their interests.

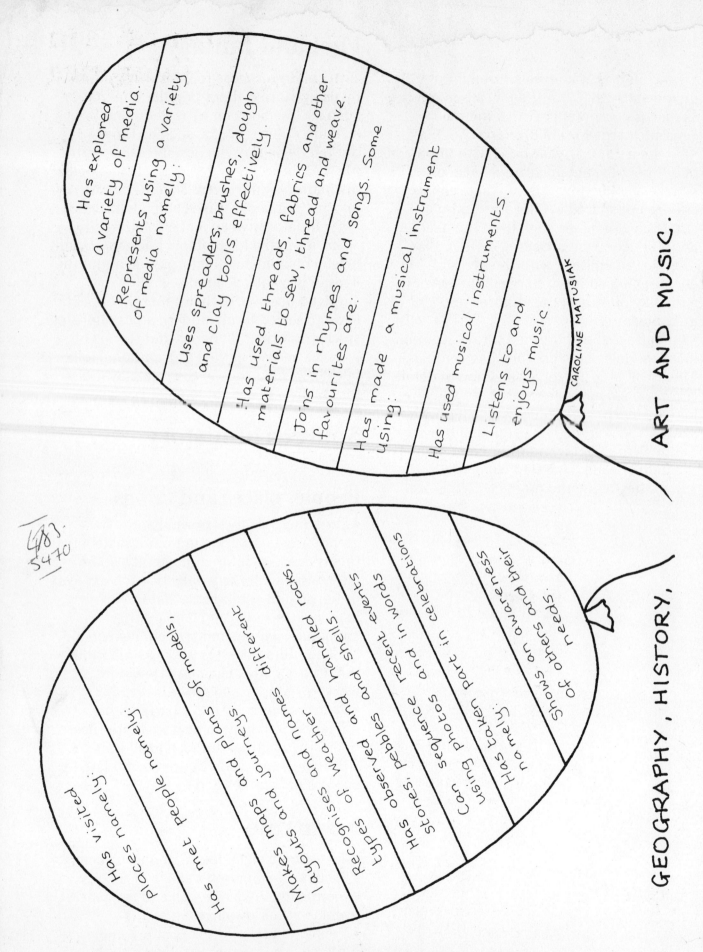

Has explored a variety of media.

Represents using a variety of media namely:

Uses spreaders, brushes, dough and clay tools effectively.

Has used threads, fabrics and other materials to sew, thread and weave.

Joins in rhymes and songs. Some favourites are:

Has made a musical instrument using:

Has used musical instruments.

Listens to and enjoys music.

CAROLINE MATUSIAK

ART AND MUSIC.

Has visited places namely:

Has met people namely:

Has made plans of models, layouts and plans namely:

Makes maps journeys: different

Recognises weather handled rocks, types observed and shells.

Has observed recent events stones, pebbles in words

sequence and celebrations

Can photos part in using by in celebrations

Has taken namely:

Shows an awareness of others and their needs.

GEOGRAPHY, HISTORY,

This page may be photocopied for use in the classroom and should not be declared in any return in respect of any photocopying licence.

176